The *Comparison* TRAP

How to Break Free, How to Stay Free

YVONNE COPELAND, MSW, LCSW

ISBN 978-1-63874-018-6 (paperback)
ISBN 978-1-63874-019-3 (digital)

Christian Faith Publishing
832 Park Avenue
Meadville, PA 16335
www.christianfaithpublishing.com

All scripture references are from the King James version of the Bible, unless otherwise stated.

Printed in the United States of America

CONTENTS

Thank you, first and foremost, to my Lord and Savior, Jesus Christ, who paid the ultimate price for my freedom (John 3:16, 8:36).

Next, a heartfelt thank you to my family, with all my love: to my ever-supportive husband, our sons and daughter-in-law, our grandchildren, my dear mom and dad and to our siblings and their families. My life is immensely richer because of each of you.

Last, but not least, in loving memory of my mother-in-law and father-in-law. Until we meet again (1 Corinthians 15:51–57).

INTRODUCTION

IF WE ARE BRUTALLY HONEST, at one time or another, most of us have had that familiar one-sided, silent, albeit sometimes inwardly blaring conversation within ourselves. You know, the one that laments, *What I wouldn't give to have her voice…his speaking ability…her sculpted body…or his popularity and disarming ability to work a room.* Or perhaps, after observing someone with the specific physical attributes we would love to have, we grudgingly question, *Why can't I be taller, shorter, darker, lighter, prettier, more good looking,* etc.? At times, those seemingly endless, self diatribes of *if only* and *what if* could go on and on, ad infinitum.

In such instances, what drives us to such intense self-scrutiny? Why do we subject ourselves to an incessant, never-ending barrage of self-defeating, questioning accusations inwardly targeted to an audience of one? And yet, at one time or another, there emerges an often unspoken dimension in virtually all of us that sees another human being and desires their looks, qualities, talents, etc. No matter our age, at some point in our lives, comparing ourselves to another invariably rears its ugly head. And in such instances, if we are candid and transparent, we call it out for what it is: insecurity, inferiority, jealousy, covetousness, envy, or conversely, it can even clothe itself as superiority and haughtiness. Regardless of the label we affix, if we are genuinely honest, some of us may go to extraordinary lengths and, in extreme cases, may even make it our life's goal to duplicate, emulate, or even strive to possess some enviable characteristic, quality, talent or material possession that belongs to another. Or instead, we may haughtily dismiss the enviable attribute of another for which, if the truth be told, we inwardly clamor.

Just why are we, as humans, prone to the proclivity of comparing ourselves to another? Or could it actually be that comparing ourselves to another is so commonplace and so accepted in our society or culture that we no longer question the veracity or consequences of such a practice? After all, how many of us, as parents, without ever considering the long-term ramifications, naively or innocently compare one of our children to the other? And in such instances where one child may have made a right decision and the other has not, the question "Why can't you be like your brother/sister?" has glibly rolled off our tongues. Maybe you have not been guilty, but I certainly have!

Google the phrase "how many ads does the average person view each day," and you will note that the average person is exposed to approximately four thousand to ten thousand ads daily. We've all heard the ploys, that is, the commercials that often surreptitiously promise: *buy this car or this new dress and you will be the envy of all!* And once enticed, some of us inadvertently pattern our lives after the often illusory facade of other family members, friends, and associates or the picturesque lifestyles of total strangers posted on Facebook we may never meet. All the while, we never stop to realize that those same individuals—often themselves seeped in their own deceptions, illusions, and/or half-truths—may simply be posting false representations of their own incomplete, unfulfilled lives.

The insightful twentieth-century theologian/pastor Dr. Adrian Rogers wisely observed that "It's about time we stopped buying things we don't need with money we don't have to impress people we don't like." His timeless truism cannot only be applied to material things but to *any* quality someone else may have that we want. Sadly, when our focus turns to others and the possessions or characteristics they possess, we may invariably never embrace or develop our own innate and distinct God-given talents and abilities. Most importantly, we unintentionally overlook our own God-ordained destiny. As a result, we unwittingly relegate ourselves to a self-defeating, never-ending striving for the unattainable, and with that self-imposed striving comes a congruent, vain attempt to imitate the demeanor, lifestyle, or God-given destiny, talent, or ability of another.

Without doubt, most of us are acutely aware of the major sins listed in the Bible. In fact, we may know some of them by heart: murder, fornication, adultery, thievery, idolatry, etc. (Matthew 19:18, 1 Corinthians 6:9–10, Revelation 21:8). But what of *comparison*? Though not explicitly mentioned in the aforementioned verses, once it obtains a foothold, the insidious, deceptive trap of comparison can in fact serve as a precursor to many other more familiar sins.

This book delves into the pitfalls of comparison and how its lethal tentacles can ever so subtly, ever so stealthily invade every part of our lives, ensnaring us. And yet a stark reality check that intentionally reminds us of the deceptive trap of comparison is only half the battle. Where do we go from there? A critical discussion of the comparison trap from a biblical viewpoint ensues in the subsequent pages of this book. Additionally, theoretical concepts from a behavioral health perspective are also intertwined in various sections of this work. Practical suggestions on how to identify and overcome the insidious strangleholds inherent in the comparison trap are also included. Finally, a specific prayer for the reader at the end of each chapter invites God's intervention and blessing into each topic discussed.

The freedom to no longer feel that we must *outdo*, that we must *out be*, and that we must *outperform* another is actually attainable. Ultimately, however, it mandates complete surrender to the reality that each of us, as human beings created in the very image of Almighty God, is afforded a viable, life-giving option. We are given the choice to either succumb to the falsehoods inherent in the comparison trap or to choose instead to wholeheartedly embrace our Father God's distinct, unique plan and purpose for each of our individual lives. However, in choosing the latter, we deliberately stave off the desire, compulsion, or predilection to compare ourselves with others.

May God use the words on each page of this book to assure you, the reader, of His steadfast love and His unique design and plan for your life so that you may know, without question or dispute, that there is no one else in this entire world like you and that you and you alone are His priceless creation. Most importantly, may you know, with full assurance, that His plan for you is good and not evil and that He has given you a future and a hope (Jeremiah 29:11)!

CHAPTER 1

The Genesis of Comparison

And the serpent said unto the woman, Ye shall not surely die: For God doth know that in the day ye eat thereof, then your eyes shall be opened, and ye shall be as gods, knowing good and evil.
—Genesis 3:4–5

MOMMA'S SAGE ADVICE OF YESTERYEAR rings just as cogently true today as it did so many decades ago when, as a little girl, she wisely advised me, "Love yourself, baby…always be who God called you to be." In short, Momma was knowingly admonishing me to be true to myself, to specifically travel my own God-ordained path in life, and to not try to live someone else's life. My mother's keen but matter-of-fact instruction represents but a snippet of the prudent counsel and common sense some of us may have gleaned at one time or another from our experienced elders as we grew up. Priceless gems of wisdom bestowed upon us as we ultimately began to navigate the corridors of our own busy, often hectic, pressure-filled lives. Over and over again throughout my life, I have had the opportunity to either follow Momma's advice of long ago or to succumb to the often subtle, enticing lure of the comparison trap.

Likewise, as a licensed clinical social worker for many years, I have at times observed a distraught client in a similar situation. In such an instance, the unwitting client before me in the therapy session may also find himself in the throes of comparison, often at odds with his own imaginary nemesis, confronting his own self-imposed challenges. As a result, the client may blindly adopt previously mistaken preconceived goals as his unrealistic yardstick. When the client accepts these blatantly false assumptions as truth, however, conflictual emotions of dismay, discouragement, and disillusionment may ensue. Consequently, the client repeatedly chastises himself that he is not where he thinks he must or should be in his current season of life.

The aforementioned client may have never embraced the reality that as God's creation, each of us is a unique, one-of-a-kind masterpiece. And that, based on this divine truth, our Heavenly Father's goals for each of us are also uniquely different. God's dreams and ultimate purpose for your life may lead you along a different pathway than His plans for my life. God's destiny for your life may be diametrically opposed to His blueprint for my life. However, for each of us to faithfully and successfully navigate our own personal, God-ordained, God-directed roadmap is tantamount to the congruent realization of a life well lived according to our Heavenly Father's extraordinary design and plan for each of us. To begin to embrace God's divine template for our individual lives, however, begins with the recognition that each of us possesses a specific MO.

MO, short for *modus operandi*, is defined in *Webster's* dictionary as "a method of procedure." In military circles, MO is an abbreviation for the designated task or job assignment initially assigned the recruit by his military branch. Within such a framework, a poignant question inevitably surfaces that demands a thoughtful response from each of us. Are you and I following our own God-given, God-designed purpose or MO for our lives, or have we swerved off course in hot pursuit of another's MO instead?

Furthermore, within the backdrop of the scriptural admonition, "Let this mind be in you which was also in Christ Jesus" (Philippians 2:5), can we begin to envision a *God-perspective* regarding the path our own individual lives are to follow? In order to intentionally avoid the comparison trap, we must periodically ask ourselves this question if we are to experience God's singular, individualized design for each of our lives, unconditionally accept ourselves, and seek to become who Creator God made each of us to be.

When I was a little girl, I can remember my two younger sisters and I sneaking into my mom and dad's bedroom and venturing into the clothes closet our parents shared. With muffled whispers and mischievous grins, we went directly to our mother's side of the closet where on the floor were neatly arrayed beautiful high heels which were briefly ours for the choosing. Three little girls trying on their mom's high heels—what a hilarious sight to behold! But as little girls, our mother, who wore her three-inch high heels with such elegance, finesse, and style, indirectly modeled for us by her own graceful strides the way we hoped to one day carry ourselves when we, as grown women, donned our own high heels.

I find it amusing now when I think back on that moment in time, but have we not all, in some period in our lives and in some form or fashion, played dress up, trying to be something we are not but perhaps that we aspire to be? And there is nothing wrong with that. However, the perspective on comparison of which I speak entails more than the childlike escapade of simply donning Mom's high heels.

Fritz Kreisler, one of the foremost violinists who ever lived, was a gifted musician who, in his youth, veered away from what he was created to do and earnestly tried to become something he was not created to do or to be. As a young man, he tried medicine and failed to finish medical school. Opting for a military career, he joined the army and failed to get promoted. He tried other ventures and, time and again, failed. However, it was only when Fritz Kreisler came to the realization that the one thing he most loved in life was music that his life changed. It was then at that point that he threw himself wholeheartedly, with complete abandon, into the pursuit of music, a discipline which imbued him with joy and with deep passion. It was then that he realized that this was what Fritz Kreisler had been created to do and to be (https://jentezenfranklin.org/daily-devotions/recognize-your-gift-know-your-goal).

As believers, our ability to hear the voice of our Lord and Savior, Jesus Christ, and to get our instructions and marching orders directly from Him is not only paramount, but it is also what brings our Father God the utmost *glory*. Scripture explains it best. As 1 Corinthians 12 clearly delineates, if our Lord made me a foot instead of a hand, that does not negate my importance in the body. However, if I, for whatever reason, decide to perform the work of a hand, rather than the work of a foot for which I was created, I am, in reality, no longer reaching my highest potential. Rather, in making such a decision, I have failed to embrace God's ultimate grand design and purpose for my life.

This brings us back to the topic of comparison, which plays its own often overlooked yet insidious role in our society and culture. Sadly, like my client that I alluded to earlier, we may often live lives so entangled in comparison's silent web that we sometimes never fully realize just how deeply entrenched and entrapped in its tentacles we have become. As a result, the subtle, often unspoken need or compulsion for us to compare ourselves to others or to strive to be like others outweighs the open, unconditional invitation from our Lord and Savior, Jesus Christ, to seek and fulfill *His* unique will and purpose for our individual lives.

Webster's dictionary defines *comparison* as "the act or process of comparing" or "likening." It defines *trap* as "something by which one is caught or stopped unawares."

In 2 Corinthians 10:12 (KJV), the apostle, Paul, strongly warns us against comparison, noting,

> *For we dare not make ourselves of the number, or compare ourselves with some that commend themselves: but they measuring themselves by themselves, and comparing themselves among themselves are not wise.*

The Life Application Bible succinctly states the same verse:

> *We do not dare to classify or compare ourselves with some of those who commend themselves. But when they measure themselves by one another, and compare themselves with one another, they do not show good sense. (2 Corinthians 10:12)*

And in yet another translation of the same verse, the Message Bible further clarifies:

> *We're not, understand, putting ourselves in a league with those who boast that they're our superiors. We wouldn't dare do that. But in all this comparing and grading and competing, they quite miss the point.*

A few verses later, the Message Bible translation soundly admonishes the reader:

> *"If you want to claim credit, claim it for God." What you say about yourself means nothing in God's work. It's what God says about you that makes the difference.* (2 Corinthians 10:17–18)

Without doubt, *comparison* is to be shunned, but an even further precipitous fall down the winding, slippery slope of comparison is to *covet*. According to *Webster's* dictionary, to covet is "to wish for enviously," "to feel inordinate desire for what belongs to another." In short, if left unbridled and uncontrolled, comparison can ultimately lead to far worse, that is, to covetousness.

So far-reaching are the negative consequences of covetousness that God included it as the fourth of the Ten Commandments He gave to the children of Israel. God declared, "Thou shalt not covet," followed by an explicit warning that "thou shalt not covet thy neighbor's house, thou shalt not covet thy neighbour's wife, nor his manservant, nor his maidservant, nor his ox, nor his ass, nor any thing that is thy neighbour's" (Exodus 20:17).

So what is it that compels us to want to be like others and/or to want what they have? If we journey back to the very beginning of Genesis, shortly after God created the first man and first woman, Adam and Eve, Genesis 1:31 records, "God saw everything that He had made, and, behold, it was *very good*" (italics, mine). In Psalm 139:14, the writer, David, further validates this as he describes himself as "fearfully and wonderfully made." These and numerous other scriptures corroborate that God made each man and each woman as *very good*, truths which clearly invalidate any need on our part to covet. And though our Heavenly Father God reiterates that once we have accepted Christ, we are "complete in Him" (Colossians 2:10), we have not yet attained our glorified bodies, and sin can still lie at the door (Genesis 4:7). Nor does the Prophet Jeremiah, in Jeremiah 17:9, gloss over the sheer magnitude of this truth, as he wisely posits and then questions, "The heart is deceitful above all things, and desperately wicked, who can know it?" But there is One who knows! Our Father God knows the heart and true condition of man, which is why He included "thou shalt not covet" in His list of life's ten most important laws.

While most of us know that it is wrong to covet, what of the spiritual gifts we observe in another? In 1 Corinthians 12:28–30, for instance, Paul lists some of the gifts resident within the body of Christ:

> *And God hath set some in the church, first apostles, secondarily prophets, thirdly teachers, after that miracles, then gifts of healings, helps, governments, diversities of tongues.*
>
> *Are all apostles? Are all prophets? Are all teachers? Are all workers of miracles?*
>
> *Have all the gifts of healing? Do all speak with tongues? Do all interpret?* (1 Corinthians 12:28–30)

However, the writer explicitly follows up this list with his admonition in verse 31 to "covet earnestly the *best* gifts" (italics mine) while, with profound revelatory insight, he adds, "and yet I shew you a *more excellent way*" (italics mine). And just what is that *way*? Specifically, Paul then points us to the *way of charity* or *love* as he powerfully pens the eloquent thirteenth chapter of 1 Corinthians. And while Paul exhorts us earlier in 1 Corinthians 11:1 to: "be ye followers of me, even as I also am of Christ," he notes that even in following him (Paul), we are, in essence, to be followers of our Lord and Savior, Jesus Christ, the foremost example and head of us all.

Consequently, other than to covet earnestly "the *best* gifts" and "the *more excellent way*" of charity or love, to unwisely compare ourselves to others and to covet what they have should never be the motivation for the choices and decisions we make.

Ah, but strive we nonetheless do and often with reckless abandon as we earnestly pursue seemingly elusive dreams that we believe will satisfy the deepest longings of our hearts. In fact, as far back as the book of Genesis, the Bible is replete with examples of the unforeseen negative consequences posed by comparison and by those who ill-advisedly compared themselves with others.

We only need to turn back in our Bibles to the earliest annals of recorded time when in the Garden of Eden, God gave Adam and Eve *everything*—everything, that is, except the choice to eat fruit from the tree of the knowledge of good and evil (Genesis 3:3). As you may recall, the serpent subtly beguiled Eve by promising her that if she would only eat of the fruit of the tree in the midst of the garden, "then your eyes shall be opened, and *ye shall be as gods...*" (Genesis 3:5, italics, mine). Enticed, Eve dared compare herself to God and to covet His position. Within Eve arose the insatiable desire for the forbidden fruit that God had previously warned her and her husband, Adam, to shun. The insidious thought planted in Eve's mind by the serpent that Eve and her husband could be "as gods," that they would dare to covet God's position and make themselves equal with God, ultimately introduced evil and sin into a heretofore spotless world that would forever alter the destiny of mankind. We all know the devastating, heartbreaking end of the story...that after eating the forbidden fruit, Adam and Eve were subsequently banished from the Garden of Eden to a lifetime of heartache, pain, toiling the ground, labor during childbirth, etc.

Unfortunately, the ramifications of comparison and its accompanying bedfellow, covetousness, did not end there. Banished from the Garden of Eden, Adam and Eve later became parents to two sons, Cain and Abel. As a young adult, Cain, a farmer, became angry and resentful when the sacrifice of Abel, a herdsman, was accepted by God, while Cain's sacrifice was not.

As the Bible recounts in Genesis, the fourth chapter, Cain brought an offering to God from the produce of his farm. Abel also brought an offering but selected the best from the firstborn animals of his herd. God accepted Abel and his offering, but Cain and his offering did not receive God's approval. In response, Cain lost his temper and went into a sulk.

Observing Cain's resentment, God questioned Cain,

> *Why this tantrum? Why the sulking? If you do well, won't you be accepted? And if you don't do well, sin is lying in wait for you, ready to pounce; it's out to get you, you've got to master it.* (Genesis 4:6–7, The Message Bible)

However, rather than *master* his jealousy, an angry and spiteful Cain responded by having words with his brother, Abel, and subsequently, in a fit of rage, took his own brother's life. As Genesis 4:3–8 in the King James Version reads in its entirety,

> *And in process of time it came to pass, that Cain brought of the fruit of the ground an offering unto the Lord.*
>
> *And Abel, he also brought of the firstlings of his flock and of the fat thereof. And the Lord had respect unto Abel and to his offering:*
>
> *But unto Cain and to his offering, he had not respect. And Cain was very wroth, and his countenance fell.*
>
> *And the Lord said unto Cain, Why art thou wroth? And why is thy countenance fallen?*
>
> *If thou doest well, shalt thou not be accepted? and if thou doest not well, sin lieth at the door. And unto thee shall be his desire, and thou shalt rule over him.*

*And Cain talked with Abel his brother: and it
came to pass, when they were in the field, that Cain
rose up against Abel his brother, and slew him.*

Like Cain, wanting what another has can surface suddenly, without warning or it can gradually surface. And it can happen, no matter our age. As parents, many of us may have seen the scenario played out repeatedly, countless numbers of times, in our own children who, rather than being satisfied with what they have, want more…they want *theirs*, namely, what someone else has. Even as a young child develops and matures and becomes more cognizant of right and wrong, previously unforeseen comparisons with others may also subtly develop. And if we, as parents, are not watchful and observant, correspondingly selfish, demanding emotions and behaviors may instinctively surface as well. As previously noted, within the first few chapters of Genesis, comparison and covetousness raised their ugly heads with, albeit, destructive consequences.

Another equally compelling illustration of the destructive consequences of comparison is recorded later in the same book of Genesis when the patriarch Jacob made Joseph, his favorite son, a coat of many colors. In doing so, the father's ill thought-out actions only further cemented the growing resentment that Joseph's brothers harbored toward their younger sibling. With each passing day, the brothers witnessed firsthand the intense, openly biased, and favored status and affection bestowed by their father upon their younger brother. In displaying such favoritism, Joseph's father, Jacob, inadvertently planted and nurtured the destructive seeds of comparison and accompanying jealousy in the minds of the resentful brothers which ultimately culminated in Joseph's staged killing by wild animals and his sale into slavery. Later, after a brief promotion to the position of manager in Potiphar's house and a subsequent, false accusation leveled at Joseph by his master's wife, Joseph found himself wrongfully imprisoned for thirteen arduous years in a dingy, damp prison (Genesis, chapters 39–41).

Sadly, the negative fallout from the comparison trap does not stop with Joseph's family. As recounted in the book of 1 Samuel in the Old Testament, a young, unassuming shepherd boy named David used a slingshot and a smooth stone to strike a deathblow to the formidable giant, Goliath. After performing such a heroic feat, the young lad, David, was soon publicly lauded for having killed his "ten thousands," while Saul, the king of Israel, suddenly became a byline—for having only killed his "thousands" (1 Samuel 18:7). Immediately, the slimy tentacles of comparison once again surfaced, and what initially began as a harmonious relationship between Saul and David quickly disintegrated into a one-sided war, with Saul, the hunter, and David, the hunted prey. David ended up running for his life as Saul, beset by his own insecurities and jealousies, perceived David as a threat to both his power and his throne and tried, on more than one occasion, to murder the young man.

Once again, the far-reaching ramifications of comparison gone awry occurred in Isaiah, chapter 14, when, as is believed by many biblical scholars, the archangel Lucifer dared to compare himself to Creator God and decided that he wanted to be like God. As scripture records,

> *How art thou fallen from heaven O Lucifer, son of the morning! how art thou cut down to the ground, which didst weaken the nations!*
> *For thou hast said in thine heart, I will ascend into heaven. I will exalt my throne above the stars of God: I will sit also upon the mount of the congregation, in the sides of the north:*
> *I will ascend above the heights of the clouds; I will be like the most High.*
> *Yet thou shalt be brought down to hell, to the sides of the pit.* (Isaiah 14:12–15)

Not satisfied with his position as minister of music in the heavenlies, scripture records that Lucifer dared compare himself to God and actually coveted God's position as he boldly proclaimed, "I will be like the most High." We are well aware that Satan did not topple our Heavenly Father off His throne. Thank our risen Savior!

However, this biblical passage does serve as a stark reminder to all of us that the deceitfulness of comparison has been present and in operation for thousands of years, even prior to the creation of Adam and Eve.

If only the previously mentioned biblical narratives involving Adam and Eve, Cain and Abel, Joseph and his brothers, David and Saul, and the fallen archangel, Lucifer, were simply isolated examples of comparison gone sadly askew. Unfortunately, the comparison trap is both subtle and far-reaching. The Bible is replete with vivid illustrations of the dire results and fallout that may occur once an individual becomes entangled in the slimy tentacles of comparison.

Throughout both the Old and New Testament, the biblical writers cite vivid examples of the inherent pitfalls of comparison. For example, in the New Testament, a glaring instance of the comparison trap unfolds in the story of the prodigal son, who unintentionally steals the spotlight from his older brother with his ultimate return home in disgrace. As the parable unfolds in Luke 15:11–32, the prodigal son, irrefutably a rebel armed with his own agenda, demanded his inheritance and left home for a far country where he spent all that he had. Yet when he eventually returned home a pauper, his father ran out to meet him. The elder man lovingly kissed his younger son, placed a ring upon his finger, killed and cooked a fatted calf and threw the now humble, contrite, rag muffin son an elaborate party fit for royalty. To say that the older brother had a problem with this exquisite treatment of his younger brother is an understatement! Nor did the older brother—jealous and disgusted—attempt to hide his obvious disdain at the grand fanfare bestowed upon his younger, formerly wayward brother by their grateful and elated father. Scripture seemingly paints the picture of a devoted, loving father who no doubt had himself spent many a sleepless night praying ceaselessly for his prodigal son's return. The older brother, however, did not share his father's unwavering acceptance and unconditional forgiveness for his previously rebellious younger brother. As the older brother compared his father's daily treatment of him to the grand regalia now bestowed upon his younger brother, he vehemently complained. The resentful older brother pointed out that unlike his younger brother, he had never left home but had remained a faithful worker in his father's business. And yet as the older devoted brother, he had never received the celebratory applause now so lavishly heaped upon the prodigal son.

Some might dare to assert that Cain, Joseph's brothers, King Saul, the prodigal son's older brother, and other like-minded characters that various passages in the Bible so aptly depict, all remained well within their rights to react as they did, their actions seemingly justified. In fact, I am sure that each of us could identify with one, several, or perhaps with all the perspectives of the biblical characters herein discussed.

But were they within their rights to be indignant? Perhaps Jesus best addresses this question in his conversation with His disciple Peter in the book of St. John, chapter 21, shortly after He arose from the dead:

So when they had dined, Jesus saith to Simon Peter, "Simon son of Jonas, lovest thou me more than these?" He saith unto him, "Yea, Lord; thou knowest that I love thee." He saith unto him, "Feed my lambs."

He saith to him again the second time, "Simon, son of Jonas, lovest thou me?" He saith unto him, "Yea, Lord: thou knowest that I love thee." He saith unto him, "Feed my sheep."

He saith unto him the third time, "Simon, son of Jonas, lovest thou me?" Peter was grieved because he said unto him the third time, "Lovest thou me?" And he said unto him, "Lord, thou knowest all things; thou knowest that I love thee." Jesus saith unto him, "Feed my sheep."

"Verily, verily, I say unto thee, When thou wast young, thou girdest thyself, and walkest whither thou wouldest: but when thou shalt be old, thou shalt stretch forth thy hands, and another shall gird thee, and carry thee whither thou wouldest not."

> *This spake he, signifying by what death he should glorify God. And when he had spoken this, he saith unto him, "Follow me."*
>
> *Then Peter, turning about, seeth the disciple, whom Jesus loved following; which also leaned on his breast at supper and said, "Lord, which is he that betrayeth thee?"*
>
> *Peter seeing him saith to Jesus, "Lord, and what shall this man do?"*
>
> *Jesus saith unto him, "If I will that he tarry till I come, what is that to thee? follow thou me."* (John 21:15–22)

In the above passage of Scripture, it appears that Jesus has given Peter his marching orders, that is to "feed his sheep." However, Peter is not satisfied, but rather wants to know what the disciple John, the beloved disciple, will be tasked to do as well. *Comparison always looks at someone else.* Jesus's response to Peter is straightforward. Jesus basically cuts to the heart of the matter, asking Peter what concern it is of his what John does. Jesus then instructs Peter to turn his focus instead on the mission Jesus has for Peter to do, to be, to accomplish.

And yet for many of us, it is human nature to look around and compare ourselves to what others may be doing, saying, wearing, etc. And it may invariably become our unconscious *normal* to be in sync with what everyone else is doing. But Jesus encourages us to follow his explicit, unique, individualized plan and design for each of our lives. And perhaps this, in itself, is the most effective response to the dissonance, disconnect and division embodied by such biblical figures as Cain, Joseph's brothers, King Saul, the prodigal son's older brother, and others. Each of us is instructed to pursue a renewed mind (Romans 12:2) that foregoes comparisons and instead unabashedly embraces God's divine purpose and the personally prescribed, God-ordained assignment He has for each of us.

My Prayer

My Lord and my Savior, God, how easy it is to simply succumb to the dictates and mores of today's society. You have distinctly and undeniably shown in Your Word that the tendency for comparison and, in turn, covetousness, has been around for thousands of years, a lingering, invisible albatross around my neck that, if I let it, would seek to separate me from Your ultimate best for me. The tendency for me to compare myself with others has never been Your will for me. Help me to remember that Your thoughts are not my thoughts and that Your ways are not my ways. Instead, Your thoughts are higher than my thoughts, and Your ways are higher than my ways (Isaiah 55:8–9).

So, Lord, help me strive to follow the unique, God-given, God-ordained path You have meticulously and ever so lovingly designed for my singular life. And, Lord, let me not permit societal norms and mores to dictate the pattern or path my life must follow. Instead, let me wholly live for You and be sensitive to Your leading and guidance. Most of all, let this mind be in me which was also in You (Philippians 2:5) so that I may truly hear with spiritual ears Your thoughts, Your plans, Your ways, and Your truth for my life and respond in utmost obedience. It is in the all-powerful name of my Lord and Savior, Jesus Christ, I humbly pray. Amen.

CHAPTER 2

The Root of the Problem

And Jesus answered and said unto her, Martha, Martha, thou art careful and troubled about many things: But one thing is needful...
—Luke 10:41–42a

BAGGAGE, SO HEAVY AND OH so burdensome, and yet many of us still continue to tightly grasp these bulky, often unmanageable suitcases as, encumbered with the exorbitant, excessive weight, we journey through this brief interlude called life. How well I recall an ever-increasing accumulation of baggage as my own inadequacies and weaknesses surfaced during childhood. Though many decades have now passed, I still faintly recall images of myself as a timid elementary school student, awkward, gangly, one of the last to be chosen for the team in gym class, never quite fitting in. Almost always standing alone—before the school bell rang each morning or at recess or at lunch—I was often that solitary figure on the sidelines. Repeatedly walking through the school corridors by myself resulted in its own form of self-deprecation and self-consciousness. Such feelings of inadequacy and the unspoken conclusion of not being quite *good enough* silently, relentlessly, followed me into my teen years. Little did I know during that young, naive time in my life that God's unerring word held a bold, yet loving reassurance to my blatantly false self-assessment of myself. Simply put, the truth of scripture proclaims that "I am complete in Him" (Colossians 2:10) and that He "will never leave me nor forsake me" (Hebrews 13:5). Instead, I carried my needless baggage for years, unaware that a simple, trusting, unwavering embrace of God's word coupled with a bold application of His truths in my life would inevitably set me free from the lies and falsehoods that I had inwardly believed and accepted in childhood.

Baggage. Unless we hand carry it aboard our flight, the first thing we do upon arrival at our destination and after disembarkation is to head for the baggage claim. And then unless we have placed a ribbon, a string, or some other identifying nomenclature on our suitcase prior to previously checking it in at our departure gate, much of the luggage loaded on the conveyor belt at the arrival baggage claim may look relatively the same. Oddly, though, we know our baggage is located there…somewhere among the hundreds of other similar bags! And just as that often heavily laden airport conveyor belt slowly and methodically carries our bags and those of so many other travelers around the turnstile so, too, do we inconspicuously transport our own invisible bags. In like manner and unaware of our own entanglement in the comparison trap, we similarly carry our own heavy load of baggage on the conveyor belt of our minds as we travel through life.

Everywhere we turn, we drag our invisible baggage. Our baggage may have first accumulated in childhood, as mine did, the result of unaddressed, unresolved issues. Or our baggage may play an integral role in our identity and who we become after we enter the never before traveled, often mystifying road to adulthood. In fact, carrying our baggage may have become such a way of life for us and such a part of us that we know no other way to be. Nonetheless, no matter when our baggage surfaced, though it may not be blatantly obvious to others, our baggage may place such an inordinate and often unbearable weight upon us that it may eventually become difficult, painful and even overwhelming to successfully maneuver or navigate our way through life. In fact, our baggage may have become such an intrinsic part of us that we never leave home without it. For each of us, the baggage may be wrapped differently…it may come wrapped as past childhood abuse or neglect, as emotional wounds or betrayal, as deliberate, intentional abandonment, or much worse. The list goes on and on. And though we may discreetly try to hide it, we may unconsciously carry our baggage with us each time we venture out into the world, so much so that it instinctively becomes part of the automatic prism through which we view our lives.

With our baggage held tightly in both hands, we may have surmised that a high income will solve all of our life's problems. After all, Solomon, the wisest man in the world, stated, "…money answereth all things" (Ecclesiastes 10:19). But as we get older, we may have also congruently begun to observe that while money addresses the symptoms—that is, our cold, hard cash immediately pays the monthly mortgage and utility bill, buys the groceries, fills the gas tank, etc.—that same green stuff neglects to address the *root cause* of our financial woes or other underlying physical, emotional, spiritual challenges, such as our ongoing discontentment, depression, marital conflict, loneliness, rejection, etc.

The Prophet Isaiah once observed, "And he shall snatch on the right hand, and be hungry; and he shall eat on the left hand, *and they shall not be satisfied*; they shall eat every man the flesh of his own arm" (Isaiah 9:20; italics mine). It's as if even though we have enough, it still doesn't satisfy us. Contrariwise, Paul boldly declares that "godliness with contentment is great gain" (1 Timothy 6:6). Or as the Message Bible translates this same verse in everyday language, "A devout life does bring wealth, but it's the *rich simplicity of being yourself before God*" (italics mine). However, if we are entangled in the comparison trap, it can be difficult to grasp the magnitude of this profundity, that is, the wealth found in literally *being yourself before God*.

But even if the aforementioned symptoms are promptly addressed, the *root cause* for our inner turmoil may itself be repeatedly overlooked. In short, just as weeds continue to grow in a yard, it is not until the root system of the weed is completely extracted or destroyed that the weed itself (the by-product or symptom) also disappears.

And so it is with our lives and with any issue or challenge that keeps us from becoming all that God has designed us to be. It is not until we identify and subsequently address and destroy the root system of the weeds that resulted in our unwanted baggage in the first place, that the weeds themselves begin to die. Then and only then, do the symptoms that continuously plague us, also die. For, if left untreated, the weeds invariably destroy other nearby healthy fruit. It is only when the root system of the weed is completely extracted, that we can begin to experience true freedom.

With the spotlight squarely on each of us, can we begin to carefully weed our own garden and identify the unwanted wild weeds that may have grown unattended, that is, the baggage we may have unintentionally carried throughout our lives from one place to another?

To extricate ourselves from the comparison trap mandates that we purposely weed through what we previously considered so important and so urgent, that is, our "must haves," and begin to earnestly identify what is truly needful in our lives; but this time, intently examined within the penetrating, illuminating light of God's Word.

In taking the above first bold step, we, in effect, begin to free ourselves from the comparison trap and no longer look to the lives of others as a yardstick for our own accomplishments or lack thereof. If you and I initiate this critical first step, we may begin to view our circumstances and our lives from a totally different perspective. It was the young David who, unimpeded and without blinders, refused to accept defeat and accurately identified the giant for who he *really* was…"this uncircumcised Philistine" (1 Samuel 17:26).

While the intentional actions to discard the baggage, to refuse to accept the status quo, to redefine ourselves and the situation are all critical to get to the root of the problem, the implementation of such bold steps may often represent unchartered territory for many of us. As a result, we may ponder how we can possibly overcome the enemy, the conflict, the roadblock before us. As I reflect on my own childhood, I can still recall a time in which I faced one of many of my own seemingly insurmountable obstacles. In one such instance, while in middle school, my youngest sister found herself the target of bullying by an older girl at the school. The bully happened to be the same age as me and in my grade level. I knew of this girl but had never had any interactions with her as we each traveled in different circles.

At that time, my two younger sisters and I all attended the same fifth- through eighth-grade middle school. My youngest sister had come home after school one evening, crying and visibly shaken and upset because she had been bullied by this older girl. When my mother found out, she turned to me and told me that, as the oldest sibling, I must always protect my younger sisters and my younger brother when such instances occurred. At this stage in my life, I shied away from confrontation of any sort, but my youngest sister had been bullied, and, inwardly, I knew I had to step in and protect her. Additionally, Momma's word was law. I knew that I better confront this situation with the bully or confront a different type of wrath at home. With that in mind, I went to school the following day and purposely decided at an opportune moment to confront the bully. At midday, I spotted her, surrounded by her passel of devoted followers. I was alone, and yet I was not completely alone. The vivid memory of my little sister crying and Momma's voice continued to reverberate in my mind, *Don't let that older girl bully your little sister.*

That day on the middle school campus, as I saw the bully sauntering down the walkway with her five to six girlfriends, I mentally braced myself as I approached her. The time had come. No opportunity to back down now. I stood face-to-face with my adversary and issued my challenge.

"You have been picking on my little sister," I said boldly, surprised at my own tenacity. "If you want to pick on somebody, fight somebody your own size!"

And with that, I took off my jacket, anticipating the inevitable brawl and subsequent school suspension that I was sure would follow. This girl who had bullied my youngest sister looked back at me, astonished and almost at a loss for words. Suddenly stupefied, she hesitated and reached for words that momentarily seemed out of reach and did not easily come. Meanwhile, her friends behind her urged her on with "Oooh, fight, fight!" The bully, taken aback, slowly and quizzically responded to me with "What are you talking about? I'm not interested in fighting you or your younger sister."

Time seemed to briefly stand still. And then as if in slow motion, the bully with whom I had prepared to come to blows—and in doing so simultaneously end my middle school career—continued her walk down the school corridor, her disappointed passel of followers in tow. Confounded by the unexpected outcome, I gladly retrieved my jacket from the ground, feeling a great sense of relief. My youngest sister would no longer be the recipient of further bullying from this girl. Also, I had followed my mother's instructions and, in the process, had not experienced my dreaded, but anticipated suspension from school that day.

Unwanted baggage? An enemy too great for us? God can handle it! Just as I came to my youngest sister's defense, that's how I picture our Lord and Savior, Jesus Christ, but with unwavering boldness and authority, placing His shield of protection around us. Countless examples of Father God's protective, vigilant stance, in which He steadfastly fights on our behalf, are recorded throughout scripture (Nehemiah 4:20, 2 Chronicles chap. 20, and Psalm 24:8).

The Bible states that Christ is willing and ever ready to take from us the weight of our heavy baggage, baggage we have painstakingly taken with us everywhere we go and that we may have silently struggled with for years. His heartfelt loving plea remains, "Come unto me, all ye that labor and are heavy laden, and I will give you rest" (Matthew 11:28).

And yet to actually rid ourselves of our baggage may denote a seemingly formidable undertaking, an overwhelming, unattainable endeavor in today's culture. Though not often touted in our modern day of groupthink, *uniqueness*, an often rare and underemphasized quality that few in today's society clamor for, *is* actually a distinct part of each of our lives when Christ is our Lord and Savior. The root word *unique* is defined as "being without a like or equal." We don't have to look far to see the results of uniqueness around us. Scientists inform us that no two snowflakes are alike; rather, each is distinctly different. Nor are any two fingerprints of the billions of people who have inhabited the earth the same. Such truths should give each of us the freedom to pursue that rare quality of uniqueness—individualism—with true abandon, while congruently shedding the silent, self-imposed need for comparison or the accompanying, insatiable desire "to be like the Joneses" or like anyone else. Instead, the embrace of such knowledge frees us to maximize the authentic gifts, talents, and abilities that God has omnisciently placed within each of us.

And yet rather than celebrate our unparalleled exceptionalism, some of us, even from early childhood, succumb to the comparison trap. Consequently, rather than embrace individualism, we strive to fit in with the crowd.

And so we never come to realize that God, who made each of us to be vastly different from any other person in the world, delights in our uniqueness, in what makes us distinct, in what makes us who we are. In short, we can choose to either embrace our individuality and our uniqueness or, at the other end of the spectrum, blindly surrender to sameness and acquiesce to groupthink. The choice is ours: to choose to be one of many in a homogenous crowd or to intentionally and courageously choose to stand out, to stand apart.

Albeit with some exceptions, for decades, modern societal culture has increasingly ascribed to groupthink, that is, wearing the same clothes, having the same viewpoints, donning the same styles and mindsets as our peers, etc. And when you or I fail to follow those accepted trends or mindsets, and we deliberately decide to be different, we run the risk of being labeled an outcast and/or experiencing ostracism from others.

The bottom line is that uniqueness will always diametrically oppose itself to groupthink. Therefore,

*the second critical step to flee the comparison trap requires a
stubborn tenacity to deliberately recognize and choose to embrace
our uniqueness and what makes each of us who we are.*

That means we intentionally choose *not* to compare ourselves to another. That means that we intentionally choose *not* to long or pine for what others may so easily, unabashedly embody or represent. Rather, we choose instead to intentionally focus on becoming our authentic, true selves for, throughout the vast expanse of this amazing universe, there is no one else like you and there is no one else like me. God made each of us distinct, unique and one of a kind!

My Prayer

By faith, Lord, I ask that You remove from me any baggage that I have knowingly or unknowingly taken with me as I have traveled this life's journey. Lord, thank You for the magnifying glass of Your love shining brightly on my until now, hidden baggage and on the root of the problems in my own life. Thank You, Lord, that, with your help, I henceforth no longer allow other people or even my circumstances to define me. Instead, from this day forward, I place all my baggage and all my cares on Your shoulders. Heal me from my often unseen, unspoken, invisible, and yet ever-present wounds.

Lord, hauling unwanted baggage from place to place has prevented me from seeing me as You see me. But I unabashedly thank You right now for the unique gifts, talents, and abilities that You have given to me, to include those previously hidden, dormant gifts, talents, and abilities that I may have overlooked or dismissed. Help me to begin to refer to myself as You refer to me as "fearfully and wonderfully made," even during those times when I may not see or feel that I am. (Psalm 139:14)

Father God, you referred to Abraham as the "father of many nations" when, as yet, he had no children (Genesis 17:5). You referred to Gideon as a "mighty man of valor" (Judges 6:12) when he had not yet fought or won in battle. Lord, help me to remember that it's not about how I feel or even what I see, for You see what I can become.

It's about Your Holy Word, the Bible, and it's what You say about me that matters. And so, Lord, help me to walk in my uniqueness and to be all that You have specifically called me to do and to become. It is in the mighty, exalted name of Jesus Christ I pray. Amen.

CHAPTER 3

The Sting of Rejection

And there is a friend that sticketh closer than a brother.
—Proverbs 18:24

IN ADDITION TO LUGGING AROUND our unwanted baggage, some of us become unwitting casualties of the comparison trap via the biting sting of rejection. As a little girl in elementary school, I can remember coming home from school on more than one occasion sobbing the words, "Mom, they don't like me" ("they" referred to certain classmates, specifically, the *popular* kids in school). Admittedly, while many of my peers appeared to quickly adjust and adapt, at that time in my young life I seemed to lack the requisite social skills so necessary in eliciting simple childhood friendships. It was only as I grew older that I wisely began to observe the unadorned truth…that friendships can sometimes be fickle, without rhyme or reason, and that it is not necessary for you or I to perpetrate any wrongdoing to be the brunt of name calling or to be disparaged or overlooked for no apparent reason.

As the writer of the book of 1 Samuel records, King Saul, deeply mired in the comparison trap, hated David "because the Lord was with him and was departed from Saul" (1 Samuel 18:12). So when King Saul foolishly compared himself to David, Scripture recounts that, from King Saul's own jealous heart sprang rancor, animosity and gratuitous violence, aimed squarely at young David. In effect,

King Saul, enmeshed in his own insecurities, became his own worst enemy. And in the final analysis, the ultimate threat to Saul's power actually lay within Saul himself. Try as David might, there was nothing that he could conceivably do to sway Saul's hostility and negative opinion of him. In 1 Samuel 24:17–21, Saul acknowledged that David had done him no wrong, noting that "thou art more righteous than I: for thou hast rewarded me good, whereas I have rewarded thee evil." And again in 1 Samuel 26:21, Saul admitted, "I have sinned; return, my son, David: for I will no more do thee harm, because my soul was precious in thine eyes this day: behold, I have played the fool, and have erred exceedingly." In each of these instances, however, though King Saul retreated and returned to his own home, he never extended friendship or reconciliation to his son-in-law, David.

As for you and me, we may never garner the approval or favor of others. And if we should supposedly procure their favor, that *favor* may, in fact, be only temporary, for a season or even worst case, disingenuous.

But who wants to be alone, on the sidelines, you may ask, as have I? Personally, as a child and young adult, I detested sitting alone in a public place. In such instances, in my own mind, it was as if there was an invisible neon sign affixed to me that screamed: *unwanted, not good enough, rejected, loser!* But that is not nor has it ever been God's definition of you or of me, so why blindly accept such a blatantly false definition of ourselves? Do we not lie to ourselves if we accept or believe such erroneous statements? How much more accurate instead to embrace the validity of God's definition of us, for even God's Son, our Lord and Savior, Jesus Christ, was not always accepted. In the end, the Sanhedrin tried him, and the Romans killed him, assuming that would be the end of His story. But it was not the end of His story, nor is it the end of ours!

As a young, impressionable youth, I was not always aware of the inerrant truth of God's Word nor of the immense power resident within the personal, powerful application of life-changing scripture and I am not alone. Leah, an often overlooked biblical character and the first wife of Jacob was quite familiar with feelings of inadequacy and rejection. Needless to say, when she *compared* herself to her stunningly gorgeous younger sister, Rachel, to say that Leah was found lacking was an understatement. The Bible describes Leah as "tender eyed" (Genesis 29:17). She was *not* beautiful and well-favored, like her younger sister, Rachel, with whom Jacob was smitten and madly in love.

You may well remember the story. Jacob, naively thinking that he was working for seven years for Rachel, the love of his life, was tricked and, on his wedding night, was given Leah, instead of Rachel, to be his bride. Though he worked an additional seven years to obtain Rachel's hand in marriage, he never loved Leah the way he loved her younger sister, Rachel. Scripture states that "when the Lord saw that Leah was hated, he opened her womb" (Genesis 29:31). With the stain of rejection upon her, Leah thought that surely, Jacob would love her more if she gave him children. But though she bore her husband seven children (six sons and a daughter), he did not love her more.

In this instance, the comparison trap wrapped its unwieldy tentacles around both of Jacob's wives, Leah *and* her sister, Rachel. For even Rachel, who unequivocally garnered the love and unwavering adoration of her husband, Jacob, likewise *compared* herself to her older sister, Leah. Scripture indicates that Rachel envied her sister, as Genesis 30:1 notes:

> *And when Rachel saw that she bare Jacob no*
> *children, Rachel envied her sister; and said unto*
> *Jacob, give me children or else I die.*

While entangled in the comparison trap, abiding contentment and genuine joy remain elusive and unattainable, as was the case with both Rachel and Leah. Neither sister realized tranquility or peace while ensnared in the slippery clutches of comparison. Rather, each sister endured their own form of rejection: that is, Leah bore the rejection of her husband's lack of love and affection toward her, while Rachel assumed the rejection and stigma associated with barrenness and her inability to bear children. And yet, God always has the final word. God chose the older of Rachel's two sons, Joseph, who would one day become second-in-command of all of Egypt (Genesis 41:40–41) and thereby save the children of Israel from starvation and extinction (Genesis 45:5–7; Genesis 50:20). And though rejected by her husband, God chose one of Leah's sons, Judah, through whom the Savior of the world, would come (St. Matthew 1:2). Though we may be rejected by others in life, we can always find solace that we are "accepted in the beloved" (Ephesians 1:6) by the One who matters most. And He has the final say in how our story ends (Jeremiah 29:11).

How comforting to know that our Heavenly Father has promised that He will never leave us nor forsake us (Hebrews 13:5). In fact, the only time that God ever forsook any of His children was when He, in a lone, solitary moment, while Jesus Christ lay hanging on a cross on Calvary, withdrew Himself from His only begotten Son (Matthew 27:46; Mark 15:34). For that singular moment, in the annals of time and within the recorded history of all mankind, the despised, rejected figure, Jesus Christ, took upon Himself the vast, innumerable sins of lost humanity. When rejection confronts us, rather than looking horizontally for others to fulfill our desires and to meet our deepest need, we can look vertically, heavenward, to our Father God, with a heart of praise. Only He can meet our deepest needs and desires and fill the wide chasm that rejection, no matter its form, may invariably bring.

And herein lies the third step out of the comparison trap,
that is, recognition and acceptance of the infallible truth
that only our Father, God, can meet our deepest needs.

When the sting of rejection brings with it the unhealthy coping mechanism of comparison, we may unintentionally find ourselves striving for the wrong things. For instance, we may find ourselves trying to achieve love through performance as did Leah who erroneously assumed that the birth of more sons to her husband, Jacob would, in turn, ignite genuine, heartfelt love and feelings of devotion toward her.

Unable to measure up in one area, comparison may lead us to explore other venues where we may falsely assume success is finally guaranteed. For instance, throughout my school career, I was always very studious. Actually, I was a perfectionist, to the point where I threw away many a sheet of notebook paper if it had even the slightest error or mistake on it. Despite my overly conscientious habits, I still awaited, with fear and trepidation, the proverbial distribution of report cards from school every six weeks. Nor did things change when I eventually entered the workforce and yearly performance appraisals and evaluations were announced. What further encumbered this already stringent process was the requirement that I write up my own self-performance evaluation, submit it, and then await my supervisor's subsequent annual assessment of my performance.

Performance appraisals, performance evaluations, performance reviews, report cards—all reinforce our erroneous inner belief that performance is always inextricably woven to reward. And yet, in many instances, it is, for as the apostle Paul wisely reminds us, as we sow, so shall we also reap (Galatians 6:7).

However, in the grand tapestry of our lives and viewed through the prism of comparison, is it ultimately what others think of us or say about us or write about us that eventually matters most? Or, from a much different perspective, is it what we accomplish with what we have been given and what our Father God says about us that is of utmost importance? Additionally, can any external person or entity truly assess if we have performed our duties or responsibilities at our maximum potential? Our supervisor or others in authority may attribute to us an accurate or an inaccurate assessment of our performance based on the limited information at their disposal. However, it is Almighty God who sees the intent of our hearts and our level of ability, motivation and passion, and only He can most accurately assess or measure the results and reward us accordingly (Jeremiah 17:10).

God's Word spotlights the import of recognizing the ulterior motives that underlie our actions and performance. Colossians 3:23–24 admonishes, "And whatsoever ye do, do it heartily as to the Lord, and *not* unto men; Knowing that of the Lord ye shall receive the reward of the inheritance: for *ye serve the Lord Christ"* (italics, mine). Consequently, if we really perform *as unto the Lord*, to please and honor an audience of One, our Heavenly Father, then our expectation is from Him alone. For He is the ultimate rewarder, and He will give us our just reward. Man may or may not reward or compensate us or even acknowledge our efforts. However, God sees our heart, our motives, and our intent, and He promises that He will reward us accordingly (Matthew 16:27).

Undoubtedly, at the central core of every matter, every action, lies the underlying intent or motivation that prompted it. Why do we do what we do? If we do what we do to win approval, to earn respect, to hear the praises of man, then as St. Matthew succinctly notes, that is our reward (Matthew 6:5).

James 2:20 declares that faith without action or works is dead. God looked with approval upon the unwavering, resolute act of obedience of Abraham as He said to this patriarch and future father of nations: "Now I know that thou fearest God, seeing thou hast not withheld thy son, thine only son from me" (Genesis 22:12).

Abraham could have repeatedly stated that he trusted God, but it was in Abraham's outward obedience, in his actions, in not withholding his son of promise, from a seemingly, inevitable sacrificial death on an altar of fire that visibly proved Abraham's unshakeable, abiding belief that God was first. Not even Abraham's beloved, cherished son meant more to Abraham than his relationship with Father God. From Abraham's sincere, heartfelt actions, he revealed to God not only the inner workings of a faith-filled heart, but he showed that God was truly the foremost, number one priority in his life. As Romans 4:3 declares, "For what saith the scripture? Abraham believed God, and it was counted unto him for righteousness."

Sometimes, especially when we are entangled in the comparison trap and it seems like *everybody else is doing it* and *everybody else is wearing that style* and *everybody else is going there*, it just seems so much easier to go with the flow. In such instances, it seems much more comfortable to just live with less than optimal choices than to wrest ourselves from comparison's often subtle grip. It is much easier to resign ourselves to *that's just the way I am* or *that's just the way it is.*

But that's never God's way. By His strength and grace, let it not be our way. Eternal rewards await the God pleaser, rather than the man pleaser. As Paul pointedly asks in Galatians 1:10, "For do I now persuade men, or God? Or do I seek to please men? For if I yet pleased men, I should not be the servant of Christ." This verse serves as a somber reminder to each of us to continue to actively, aggressively fight the allure and subsequent stranglehold of comparison.

My Prayer

Lord, it is inevitable. If I live long enough, I will experience some form of rejection. But in the midst of any rejection I may encounter, let me remind myself that You do not reject me. Your invitation to me is always, "Come unto me, all ye that labor and are heavy laden and I will give you rest" (Matthew 11:28). You lovingly remind me that Your yoke is easy and Your burden is light (Matthew 11:30).

Once again, thank You, Lord, for the reassurance that I am "accepted in the beloved" (Ephesians 1:6), accepted by the One who matters most. Lord, help me to never forget that only You can meet my deepest needs. When rejection does come, comfort me with Your assurance that You are ever with me, that You will never leave me nor forsake me (Hebrews 13:5), and that You, Lord, stick closer than even a brother (Proverbs 18:24). Thank You for hearing my petitions and for answering them. It is in the matchless, magnificent name of my Lord and Savior, Jesus Christ, that I pray. Amen.

CHAPTER 4

False Barometers of Success

This book of the law shall not depart out of thy mouth but thou shalt meditate therein day and night, that thou mayest observe to do according to all that is written therein: for then thou shalt make thy way prosperous, and then thou shalt have good success.

—Joshua 1:8

As a high school freshman, I can still remember Dad attending one of my girls' basketball team's games, held during a weeknight after school in the high school gymnasium. On that particular evening, out of the corner of my eye, I saw him quietly enter the gym and effortlessly climb to the middle section of the almost empty bleachers. I could tell from my quick side glances that his gaze remained steadfastly fixed on me as he intently watched me play throughout the game's entirety. I wasn't a very good basketball player (I only scored two points during the entire game), but I didn't care. My dad had come to see me play, and I was on cloud nine!

As youngsters, we boldly, unapologetically clamor for attention. "Mom, look at me!" "Dad, look, look!" we shout as we proudly show off some new daring feat or perform some innovative, never-before-seen, never-before-attempted, pioneering exploit or endeavor. And once those solicited glances are ours and ours alone, we revel with excitement and pride as our audience of one or two will gaze, sometimes with rapt attention and at other times with feigned admiration, upon our antics or the new achievements or skills we recently acquired.

Perhaps like some of you, when I reflect on my own childhood, youth, and the self-absorbed world in which I was center stage, I often envisioned surpassing lofty benchmarks by the time I attained certain ages. But what role does comparison play in each of our lives when we do grow up but may have never accepted our authentic selves? In short, if we have not embraced who we are, that gnawing desire for affirmation lingers and can stealthily follow us into adulthood with the same unrelenting intensity as our own shadow. Instead of "Look, Mom, look!" in its grown-up version, the verbiage becomes "Mom, just wanted to let you know that I received a promotion!" or "Dad, my boss says I'm one of the best workers he has!" Though they may be matter-of-fact statements now, rather than the giddy child-like proclamations of yesteryear, the inner responses hoped for may still sound eerily familiar…"please affirm me, tell me I'm doing well, that I'm important, that I matter."

Without doubt, no matter how old we get, we want affirmation, to know that we matter, that what we accomplish matters, that we are successful. In my role as a therapist, I recall speaking with a forty-two-year old woman who, with tears streaming down her face, confessed, "What I wouldn't give to hear my parents say 'I'm proud of you.'"

So how do we measure this long sought-after, but often elusive, nonquantifiable concept of *success*? Better yet, how do we know when we have achieved it? After all, is not that the end goal of comparison: to successfully acquire or mirror the characteristics, traits, or qualities of another, or conversely, to disparage someone who fails to obtain, realize, or mirror those characteristics, traits, or qualities?

Perhaps, first and foremost, we must understand and accept that the world's idea of success is *not* God's idea of success. In one biblical passage, Jesus recounts an instance in which the rich and wealthy cast lavish sums of money into the offering plate while a poor widow threw in just two mites (Mark 12:41–44; Luke 21:1–4). Yet Jesus commended the poor widow for her giving rather than the wealthy, noting that she had cast in more than the rich, for she held back nothing but gave *all* she had.

Through the stilted lens of comparison, we can never attain an accurate gauge of success. By looking at others, what they possess and what they have acquired, we may unintentionally use inequitable modes of measurement as we compare their achievements to our own.

In Matthew 25:14–30, Jesus explicitly likens the kingdom of heaven to

> *a man travelling into a far country, who called his own servants, and delivered unto them his goods.*
>
> *And unto one he gave five talents, to another two, and to another one; to every man according to his several ability; and straightway took his journey.*
>
> *Then he that had received the five talents went and traded with the same, and made them other five talents.*
>
> *And likewise he that had received two, he also gained other two.*
>
> *But he that had received one went and digged in the earth, and hid his lord's money.*
>
> *After a long time the lord of those servants cometh, and reckoneth with them.*
>
> *And so he that had received five talents came and brought other five talents, saying, Lord, thou deliveredst unto me five talents: behold, I have gained beside them five talents more.*
>
> *His lord said unto him, Well done, thou good and faithful servant; thou has been faithful over a few things I will make thee ruler over many things: enter thou into the joy of thy lord.*
>
> *He also that had received two talents came and said, Lord, thou deliveredst unto me two talents: behold, I have gained two other talents beside them.*

His lord said unto him, Well done, good and faithful servant; thou has been faithful over a few things, I will make thee ruler over many things: enter thou into the joy of thy lord.

Then he which had received the one talent came and said, Lord I knew thee that thou art an hard man, reaping where thou hast not sown, and gathering where thou hast not strawed.

And I was afraid, and went and hid thy talent in the earth; lo, there thou hast that is thine.

His lord answered and said unto him, Thou wicked and slothful servant, thou knewest that I reap where I sowed not, and gather where I have not strawed:

Thou oughtest therefore to have put my money to the exchangers, and then at my coming I should have received mine own with usury.

Take therefore the talent from him and give it unto him which hath ten talents.

For unto everyone that hath shall be given, and he shall have abundance: but from him that hath not shall be taken away even that which he hath.

And cast ye the unprofitable servant into outer darkness: there shall be weeping and gnashing of teeth.

While the parable of the five, two, and one talents delineates the importance of utilizing to the fullest extent possible the gifts that God has graciously bestowed upon each of us, there remains another significant meaning sometimes overlooked in this scriptural passage. This concerns the distribution of the talents. To one, the master gave five talents, to another, two talents, and to a third, he gave one talent. The master wanted each servant to work with what each had been given, with the expectation that each would multiply their specific talents/abilities. Thus, the two servants who had been given the five talents and two talents, respectively, were no better than the servant who had been given the single talent. However, the first two servants worked earnestly to *multiply* what they had been given and, as a result, received praise from their master whereas the servant with the one talent buried his talent and was soundly chastised. He was berated not because he had only been given one talent but because he *did nothing* with the one talent he had been given. As Matthew 25:25–27 notes, at the very least, he could have placed his money in the bank where it could have accrued interest. Instead, he buried his talent. Again, it was not the number of talents each of the servants received but rather, what each servant did to multiply or increase their talent/ability that ultimately mattered.

If we are to successfully wrest ourselves from the comparison trap, the fourth salient point challenges us:

> *To purposely refuse to imitate or adopt the attributes,*
> *qualities, talents, etc. that our all-wise God has bestowed*
> *on others as the "gold standard" for our own success.*

In short, what are we doing with what God has given to each of us? If our definition of success is spotlighted through the faulty lens of comparison and is based on the perceptions, possessions, or inherent qualities of others rather than on our own individual gifts, talents, and abilities, we will never realize or come to appreciate the innate qualities resident within us. Instead, we will falsely embrace others' definition of us and apply their erroneous, often-misplaced definition of *success* to our own lives.

What happens when we experience freedom from the entanglement and bondage of the comparison trap and the continual striving to emulate others? What does *real* success from such a vantage point look like?

Webster's dictionary defines *success* as "1: outcome, result, 2a: degree or measure of succeeding, b: a favorable termination of a venture; specifically, the attainment of wealth, favor, or eminence." The first part of the definition of success, that is, "outcome, result," does not automatically produce the outward display of "wealth, favor or eminence" recorded in the second part of the definition. In other words, per definition number one, success is not an automatically *quantified* entity. Rather, the "outcome, result" can be small, inconsequential, or conversely, it can be far-reaching, extensive, boundless, etc.

Within such a framework, then, it cannot be unequivocally stated, as popular culture often asserts, that money, fame, fortune, status, and power *always* represent the primary determinants of success. Contrariwise, if this were the case, would not the definition of success be in direct contradiction to the same media outlets who announce the sudden, unforeseen deaths of rich and famous men and women who unexpectedly took their own lives? Their outward *success* apparently did not circumvent the extreme, internal, irreconcilable conflict and turmoil that ultimately resulted in their own tragic suicide and demise.

Invariably, an accurate, all-encompassing definition of success is based on the firm, unwavering truth of God's Word. In Joshua 1:8, the Old Testament writer, Joshua, illumines our pathway to success as he writes,

> *This book of the law shall not depart out of thy mouth, but thou shalt meditate therein day and night, that thou mayest observe to do according to all that is written therein: for then thou shalt make thy way prosperous and <u>then thou shalt have good success</u> (underline, mine).*

According to Joshua, the blueprint for *good success* is *not* found in comparing ourselves to others, nor is it found in the latest fad in Hollywood, on the latest television series, or on Facebook. Nor is it found in a hefty bank account, in a glamorous house, a fine sports car, or expansive lands. Rather, *good success* is found in the pages of scripture, that is, through meditating on God's Word, the Holy Bible, day and night (Joshua 1:8) and incorporating His word into every facet of our daily lives.

And yet, this infallible and perhaps for some, unpopular truth alone calls for a referendum in which we revisit the modern-day definition of success. Though our culture highly esteems popularity, acceptance, scores of friends, etc. as essential to any modicum of success, perhaps there is something to be said for embracing the *alone* times with our Heavenly Father as opportunities to encounter Him and to experience "good success" in a far deeper, more intimately, personal realm. Conceivably, doing so represents a clear mandate that we deliberately replace the hustle and bustle of our frenetic lives with a time of contemplation and appreciation for who our Father God truly is and that we seek His incomparable plan and divine purpose for each of our lives. With God at the helm of our lives, leading and guiding us, we can experience a calm realization that it is alright to differ from others around us and to walk to the beat of a different drummer, namely, *His* drumbeat. An unexplainable peace is ours when we choose to march to the drumbeat of our master, completely in step and in sync with His distinct plan and purpose for our lives.

Based on the biblical definition of *success*, previously referenced in Joshua 1:8, coupled with *Webster's* dictionary definition of *success*, how do we begin to measure success in our own lives? For some, success may still specifically denote wealth, position, status, power, significance, popularity, etc. And while each viewpoint is totally subjective, how we each view success remains critical to the subsequent priority we give it in our lives.

Perhaps most ironic is when we erroneously base our definition of success on the opinions of others. When that happens, our concept of success is no longer firmly rooted, but instead its definition often remains fluid, ever changing, and basically unsustainable.

For example, whatever happened to some of the *successful* stars, TV series, movies, books, fashion designs that were so *in* a year ago? Many have come and many have gone. In other words, if we base our definition of *success* on the latest hit, then *success* becomes fleeting at best, that is, only relevant until that latest hit is no longer number one on the pop chart list.

If external factors become the prism through which we view success, how do we indefinitely sustain such a perspective that, in turn, unduly influences our actions, our behaviors, our philosophies, etc.?

Perhaps a more realistic definition of success is *not* one that changes with each passing fad but rather one that endures the test of time. Such a definition of *success* is not relegated to circumstances. Rather, despite the test of time and the inequities of life, the tenets of its meaning endure. Nor does this definition of success succumb to external circumstances, for external circumstances come, and external circumstances go, and yet such changes do not automatically mandate a change in our definition of success.

Or, is my definition of success predicated on how others view me? If I receive their applause, adulation and affirmation but, in doing so, unwittingly compromise my own belief system, am I really successful?

Additionally, what are clear external indicators of success? For example, in current society, without question, brand names denote importance, prestige, affluence. We proudly display the names of the manufacturer on our clothes, on our hats, on our shoes, on our cars, and even on our eyewear. Some of us go to great lengths and even spend exorbitant amounts of money for *the* name, that is, a Porsche, a Mercedes-Benz, a Rolex, a Lexus, a Louie Vuitton, a Gucci, a Calvin Klein. After all, comparison usually encompasses a significant degree of awareness. To some extent, we are cognizant of the object of our comparison, that is, some material object, some trait, quality, etc. we may have observed in another during a social interaction, while on Facebook, watching TV, etc.

But do the *names* we attach so much significance to really denote success?

For instance, I'm very sensitive about my birth name. When I initially meet someone, the first thing I want is for them to pronounce my name correctly. In fact, I think a lot of us are sensitive about our names so much so that, when we meet someone, we want them to acknowledge our individuality, our uniqueness, our distinguishing characteristics, by, for instance, remembering our name and how to correctly pronounce it.

And why even place such emphasis on my name, its correct pronunciation, its correct spelling? Could it possibly come from an innate need for recognition and acknowledgment? Ouch! I grimace as I write this! I know there have been moments in my own life when I coveted wealth and popularity. I reasoned in my younger days that if I were famous, then everyone would cry out my name in adulation. I would be a star! I would be somebody, or so I naively surmised.

The names of famous athletes, like Michael Jordan, Larry Bird, or Shaquille O'Neal, glibly roll off the lips of the television sportscaster recounting the numerous records of these sports legends or the adoring fans who continue to collect their memorabilia. No doubt their names dot the headlines of many a past sports page or biography. However, Scripture approaches this milestone or indicator of success—that is, name recognition—quite differently. For instance, as I begin to rattle off the names of the twelve disciples, of course, Simon Peter, James, John, may quickly come to mind. But how quickly does the name of James, the son of Alphaeus or Lebbaeus, whose surname was Thaddeus (Matthew 10:3), who were also Jesus' disciples, roll off the tongue? There are numerous biblical characters who, to this day, remain nameless—for example, the widow with the two mites (Mark 12:41–44), the man blind from birth (John 9:1), the prodigal son (Luke 15:11–32), etc.—but whose stories, nevertheless, profoundly affect us and point us to the unfathomable love of our Heavenly Father. Take, for instance, the woman with the issue of blood (Matthew 9:20–22) or the woman at the well (John 4:4–29) or the lad with five barley loaves and two small fishes (John 6:9) or the two thieves who hung on either side of Jesus at Calvary (Luke 23:32–43). What about the four friends who lowered the lame man through the roof (Luke 5:18–20)? All of the above represent descriptive adjectives, nouns or phrases of *anonymous* biblical characters who not only made their own indelible mark in biblical history but who also exemplified noteworthy characteristics and attributes inherent in each of us as God's creation. Rather than call them by name, we must instead satisfy ourselves with the mental image of the "great woman" (2 Kings 4:8) who built Elisha a room and whose son later died or the man by the pool of Bethesda (John 5:1–5), who had an infirmity for thirty-eight years. Did God intentionally leave out their names? Perhaps He wanted us to see a bit of ourselves in each of them. More importantly, perhaps it was not about memorializing the names of these biblical characters as it was about an up-close, personal, life-changing description of our devoted Heavenly Father, lovingly at work in the human affairs of His creation.

The Bible is replete with numerous examples of individuals who remained anonymous but whose words and actions are forever inscribed in the annals of biblical history. The Word of God is also explicit in its naming of individuals, of events, etc., often establishing a direct correlation between the name and its meaning. For example, Adam denotes *man* in Genesis 1:26 while *Eve* in Genesis 3:20 denotes *mother of all living.* Even the numbers in the Bible signify meaning. For instance, the number *7* represents completion while the number *8* signifies new beginnings.

Scripture indisputably declares, however, that the most important name in all of creation is the name of Jesus, "for there is no other name under heaven given among men, whereby we must be saved" (Acts 4:12). Jesus Christ is Emmanuel—"God with us" (Matthew 1:22–23)—and the word Christ denotes: *Messiah*, or "Anointed One" (John 1:41).

And yet the God-man, Jesus Christ, made Himself of *no* reputation (Philippians 2:7–10). Though He led a relatively obscure life, His was a life of exemplary prayer, a life of loving, sacrificial obedience to His Heavenly Father, and a life of unwavering devotion to the preordained divine path established for Him before the foundation of the world (1 Peter 1:19–20). And as the only begotten Son of the omniscient, omnipotent Eternal Father God, this one, solitary figure has continued to touch untold billions of lives for over two thousand years.

Was Jesus Christ ever enticed by comparison? The book of Matthew clearly details that Christ was led into the wilderness and tempted by the enemy three times. Two of those three occasions occurred when the enemy specifically called into question His *identity*. As noted in Matthew 4:2–11,

> *And when he had fasted forty days and forty nights, he was afterward an hungered.*

And when the tempter came to him, he said, <u>If thou be the Son of God,</u> command that these stones be made bread.

But he answered and said, It is written, Man shall not live by bread alone, but by every word that proceedeth out of the mouth of God.

Then the devil taketh him up into the holy city, and setteth him on a pinnacle of the temple.

And saith unto him, <u>If thou be the Son of God,</u> cast thyself down: for it is written, He shall give his angels charge concerning thee: and in their hands they shall bear thee up, lest at any time thou dash thy foot against a stone.

Jesus said unto him, It is written again, Thou shalt not tempt the Lord thy God.

Again, the devil taketh him up into an exceeding high mountain, and sheweth him all the kingdoms of the world, and the glory of them;

And saith unto him, All these things will I give thee, If thou wilt fall down and worship me.

Then saith Jesus unto him, Get thee hence, Satan: for it is written, Thou shalt worship the Lord thy God, and him only shalt thou serve.

Then the devil leaveth him, and behold, angels came and ministered unto him. (Matthew 4:1–11, underline, mine)

If Jesus had wanted to make a name for Himself or to showcase His power, taking Satan up on his offers would have been an obvious, inarguably, effective way to achieve those goals. Instead, His calling and election sure (2 Peter 1:10) and His assignment, clear, *Christ knew who He was.* Undaunted and undeterred, He was not beguiled by the tempter, nor did He feel the need for the approval or validation of others.

Who was this Jesus? Was He handsome, smart, debonair? According to Scripture, by today's contemporary standards, He was none of the aforementioned. In fact, the Prophet Isaiah, does not paint a flattering picture of the King of kings and the Lord of lords, noting:

> *For he shall grow up before him as a tender plant, as a root out of a dry ground; he hath no form nor comeliness; and when we shall see him, there is no beauty that we should desire him.*
>
> *He is despised and rejected of men; a man of sorrows, and acquainted with grief; and we hid as it were our faces from him; he was despised and we esteemed him not.*
>
> *Surely, he hath borne our griefs, and carried our sorrows: yet we did esteem him stricken, smitten of God, and afflicted.*
>
> *But he was wounded for our transgressions, he was bruised for our iniquities: the chastisement of our peace was upon him; and with his stripes we are healed.*
>
> *All we like sheep have gone astray; we have turned everyone to his own way; and the Lord hath laid on him the iniquity of us all.*
>
> *He was oppressed, and he was afflicted, yet he opened not his mouth: he is brought as a lamb to the slaughter, and as a sheep before her shearers is dumb, so he openeth not his mouth.*
>
> *He was taken from prison and from judgment: and who shall declare his generation? for he was cut off out of the land of the living: for the transgression of my people was he stricken.*
>
> *And he made his grave with the wicked, and with the rich in his death; because he had done no violence, neither was any deceit in his mouth.*
>
> *Yet it pleased the Lord to bruise him; he hath put him to grief: when thou shalt make his soul an offering for sin, he shall see his seed, he shall prolong*

his days, and the pleasure of the Lord shall prosper in his hand.

He shall see of the travail of his soul, and shall be satisfied: by his knowledge shall my righteous servant justify many; for he shall bear their iniquities.

Therefore will I divide him a portion with the great, and he shall divide the spoil with the strong: because he hath poured out his soul unto death: and he was numbered with the transgressors; and he bare the sin of many, and made intercession for the transgressors. (Isaiah 53:2–12)

Despite the less-than-inviting above description of our Lord and Savior, who had "no form nor comeliness" and "no beauty that we should desire him," the apostle Paul challenges us to follow in the footsteps of this Jesus who "made himself of no reputation" (Philippians 2:7). In his Epistle to the Philippians, Paul lovingly exhorts us to

let nothing be done through strife or vainglory; but in lowliness of mind let each esteem other better than themselves.

Look not every man on his own things, but every man also on the things of others.

Let this mind be in you, which was also in Christ Jesus:

Who, being in the form of God, thought it not robbery to be equal with God:

But made himself of no reputation, and took upon him the form of a servant, and was made in the likeness of men:

And being found in fashion as a man, he humbled himself, and became obedient unto death, even the death of the cross.

Wherefore, God also hath highly exalted him, and given him a name which is above every name:

> *That at the name of Jesus every knee should bow of things in heaven, and things in earth, and things under the earth;*
>
> *And that every tongue should confess that Jesus Christ is Lord, to the glory of God the Father.*
>
> *Wherefore, my beloved, as ye have always obeyed, not as in my presence only, but now much more in my absence, work out your own salvation, with fear and trembling. (Philippians 2:3–12)*

The above passage, penned by Paul, eloquently describes our Lord and Savior as confident and secure in who He was and in His God-given mission and purpose. But as for what others thought of Jesus, Matthew 16:13–17 recounts:

> *When Jesus came into the coasts of Caesarea Philippi, he asked his disciples, saying, Whom do men say that I the son of man am?*
>
> *And they said, some say that thou art John the Baptist; some, Elias; and others, Jeremias, or one of the prophets.*
>
> *He saith unto them, But whom say ye that I am?*
>
> *And Simon Peter answered and said, Thou art the Christ, the Son of the Living God.*
>
> *And Jesus answered and said unto him, Blessed art thou, Simon Barjona: for flesh and blood hath not revealed it unto thee, but my Father which is in heaven.*

Within the comparison trap, there sometimes emerges an unspoken competition or practice of outdoing or keeping one step ahead of a perceived competitor, family member, or friend. Jesus, however, never doubted who He was, nor did He question His own identity. Secure in who He was, He had nothing to prove. How many of us, on the other hand, may feel obligated to prove our importance, our significance, our reason for being to others? Or contrariwise, we feel that we must make a reputation or name for ourselves?

Like most, I've always wanted to be well-liked, well-thought of. The feedback of others, when positive, reaffirmed to me that I mattered. But what if their approval was not there? Suppose they were having a bad day themselves or failed to affirm me? Then what? Did that mean I was no longer legitimate, no longer of value? Did that mean that I no longer mattered? In the past, I permitted their validation or lack of validation to define my identity or degree of relevance.

Unmoved by the need for renown or for popularity, there are multiple instances when Jesus performed a miracle but did not want others to know (Matthew 8:4; Mark 3:12, 5:43, 7:36; Luke 5:14–16). He needed no pat on the back. If the goal of Jesus had been to make a name for Himself, He was going about it in the wrong manner.

Which begs the question, can we be satisfied to make a positive difference but without the fanfare, without the adulation of the crowd, when no one observes our act of philanthropy or our good deed, when our actions are never touted, and no one knows our name? Does it make us "less than" to *not* be in the spotlight, to *not* be the center of attention? Instead, can we be content to have the faith and confidence that Jesus Christ, our Lord and Savior, our Best Friend, is pleased with us, that He delights in us? Can we be content to await that great day when He calls our name and lovingly commends us with those long-anticipated words of approval, "Well done, thou good and faithful servant" (Matthew 25:23)?

The Bible states that our expectation should come from God alone. As Psalm 62:5 declares: "My soul, wait thou only upon God; for my expectation is from him." The Scripture clearly exhorts that, when we perform our deeds, to "do it heartily, as to the Lord, and not unto men" (Colossians 3:23). When our expectation emanates from Him alone, our intense gaze is upon Him for approval. He, the all-knowing, all-powerful judge and the ultimate rewarder, will then commend us and give us our just reward. In the final analysis, man may or may never reward or compensate us, or even acknowledge our efforts, but our eternal Father God will.

So, ultimately, does not the root cause of all action or inaction lie in our degree of motivation or lack thereof, why we do what we do? If we do what we do to win approval, to earn respect, or to hear the praises of man, then, as Matthew states, "They have their reward" (Matthew 6:2, 5, 16). If, however, we do what we do to please Almighty God, He who sees in secret will reward us openly (Matthew 6:4). Armed with such a mindset, the false narrative of comparison suddenly loses its grip and, no longer entangled in its tentacles, we experience a new level of emotional and spiritual maturity. We become like an airplane that, while in flight, rises above the turbulence of the storm, and we can begin to view firsthand the unbelievable serenity and tranquility present above the clouds. It is then and only then, that we shake off the need to be *more than*, to be *better than* and we ascend above the fray, above the need to be recognized. At such a point, we can actually stand back and observe from afar the fallout and resultant consequences that surface when comparison raises its ugly fangs and the corresponding malaise of resentment, jealousy, envy, etc. that may inevitably ensue.

This is why, rather than wallow in doublemindedness or vacillate (James 1:6-8), our Heavenly Father enjoins us to maintain singleness of heart. Quite simply when our homage is to so many others, invariably our hearts, our minds, our total devotion can never completely belong to our Lord. As a result, we walk with divided loyalty and a divided heart. And instead of wanting to wholly please our Savior and be a success in His eyes, we clamor for the approval and adulation of others whose opinions we value far more than His.

Have you noticed how certain celebrities are popular for a relatively limited amount of time, and they then fade from the elusive limelight and into obscurity? I heard a very wise woman (Momma) astutely observe, "People may put you up one day and down the next." Jesus insightfully commented on this when He boldly stated that He would not entrust or commit Himself to men "because he knew all men" and "he knew what was in man" (John 2:24–25). Movie stars, singers, and other famous personalities have their "fifteen minutes of fame," before they are cast to the side, forgotten, or seemingly overlooked, as the crowd moves on to the next big thrill.

In their programming lineup, the Sirius radio network even advertised a satellite station that spotlighted recording artists whose sole claim to fame was one major hit in their entire musical career.

Michael Jackson, Elvis Presley, Whitney Houston, and so many other stars all sought to remain relevant and to stay in the limelight. Why? Because if we are blatantly honest with ourselves, the limelight is not forever; rather, it is elusive and fleeting at best. On occasion, when I have turned on my computer, I have noticed a small sidebar appear with the headline "Hollywood stars who were once at the top of their careers and where they are now." Unfortunately for many, the once brilliant lights have dimmed, and these once sought-after stars are no longer popular or in demand. They may not have aged well, their marriages may have crumbled, their fortunes diminished, their lives now a mere whisper of what once was. Their short-lived, fleeting achievements and accomplishments seemingly become the direct antithesis of the old Christian classic which perceptively reminds us that "only what we do for Christ will last." But that goes for all of us, not just Hollywood stars. For each of us, our lives flicker but for a moment, and then they are extinguished and are no more. Psalm 90:9b may say it best, as it declares the irrefutable truth that "we spend our years as a tale that is told."

Under such a solemn decree, the foremost question for each of us remains: How do we make the brief, quickly passing moments of our lives on earth matter for eternity? Perhaps that question can best be answered in 1 Corinthians 3:7, "So then neither is he that planteth anything, neither he that watereth; but God that giveth the increase." This verse succinctly reminds us that it is not about us, but about our Father God. Consequently, a crucial key to *true success* entails a thorough, detailed exploration of who God made each of us as individuals to be and to identify how our lives can most glorify Him.

Try as we might, none of us are here to stay. Just visit a graveyard while out on a lazy, relaxing, Sunday afternoon drive. In multiple cemeteries across our vast nation, there are countless markers and tombstones, some lined in perfect rows, others not. Known only to their surviving family and friends, each gravesite is either marked or unmarked. We may recognize a name or two, but most likely, many or all the names on the markers in the cemetery are unknown to you and to me. And yet none of the deceased in any cemetery we may visit are anonymous, for each is intimately known by Father God. God Himself has proclaimed that not even a sparrow falls to the ground without His knowledge (Matthew 10:29).

Just as the markers in the countless graveyards remind us of the brevity and transitory nature of our lives, so, too, does the rapidly fleeting passage of time. Our lives, therefore, mandate that we do not linger, for even a moment on autopilot. Rather, let us continue our steadfast march forward in this life with grit, unwavering resolve and determination to fulfill our own distinct destiny—a destiny meticulously designed and preordained by our loving Heavenly Father before He formed each of us in our mother's wombs (Jeremiah 1:5).

Such undeterred, forward momentum and determined, unflinching action mandate a critical sensitivity to God's voice and to the move of God. When comparison no longer dictates our choices, we are better able to make course correction and more quickly adjust. As a result, even when the seasons of our lives change, we, too, can congruently change, and—despite the ebb and flow—follow the leading of the Spirit of God, just as Moses and the Israelites did in Exodus 13:21.

In conclusion, we can never wholeheartedly follow the cloud of God by day and the fire of God by night in our own lives if we constantly compare the trajectory of our lives with others. Conversely, however, we can begin to experience true freedom from the comparison trap via an intentional, ongoing, honest reevaluation and reassessment of *true success* through the prism of God's Word.

My Prayer

Lord, forgive me when I have so glibly bought into the lies of society's definition of success, that is, that to be happy, to be fulfilled, to "have arrived," I must have my name in lights, be rich, be popular, or possess other external trappings. Rather, help me to seek first Your kingdom and Your righteousness (Matthew 6:33). Help me to have Your servant's heart. Help me to seek Your approval and not the world's. Help me to quiet myself before You and to hear Your marching orders for my life. Help me to please You above all else so that on that Great Day, I may hear you say, "Well done, thou good and faithful servant…you have been faithful over a few things. I will make you ruler over much."

Thank You, Lord, for answering my heart's cry to experience true success in Your eyes, And it is in the matchless name of Jesus Christ, my Lord and Savior, that I pray. Amen.

Priceless: Thoughts and Talk

*A good man out of the good treasure of his heart bringeth
forth that which is good; and an evil man out of the evil
treasure of his heart bringeth forth that which is evil: for
of the abundance of the heart his mouth speaketh.*

—Luke 6:45

As a tall and gangly preadolescent eleven-year-old girl, I can still recall the short trek I made each weekday morning to the elementary school located a quarter mile from my family's home. Upon arrival, I would stand alone on what seemed like an enormous entranceway at the front of the elementary school under the wide awning, awaiting the ringing of the proverbial 8:30 a.m. school bell. Quite timid then, the other kids seemed to quickly pick up on my insecurities because every now and then, before the bell rang, I would, at times, become the brunt of snide remarks, most specifically, about my slender build. I faintly recall the jeers and the name calling, "Hey, skinny," or "Hey, skinny legs and all!" (Back then, girls were not allowed to wear slacks and jeans to school, so the dresses or skirts I wore day in and day out only highlighted my tall, obviously thin, lean frame). Shy, quiet, reserved, and unsure of myself, their name-calling only served to further diminish my fragile self-esteem.

Even the most outgoing person can feel alone at times. As a young girl, I often spent much of my free time by myself, where I would read the latest adventures of the Hardy Boys or Nancy Drew mysteries, or perhaps, I would write in my diary, immersed in my own world of make-believe. Sometimes this was my choice. At other times, however, this was the inevitable by-product of not possessing the social skills necessary to effectively converse and interact with my peers. During those awkward, uncomfortable moments of frequently standing alone most days outside that entrance to my elementary school, it seemed to me that all the other kids were laughing, talking, or absorbed in play, or so I thought. As I was promoted each year and steadily progressed through my upper elementary school years, I can still recall wondering if something was wrong with me. *Why was it so hard to make friends? Why didn't I fit in?*

Fast forward several decades later. While on an out-of-town business trip on behalf of the company for which I worked at the time, I made a pilgrimage back to that city of my childhood. While there, I made it a point to drive by the school that had, for many years since, always brought back a flood of overwhelmingly negative memories and painful emotions. However, when I finally found the address and drove up to the school in my rental car, I experienced stark amazement! Over those several decades, the huge daunting portal to my elementary school had suddenly, mysteriously diminished in size, and the once looming, formidable entranceway to the school that for years had towered menacingly in the recesses of my mind each time I reflected back on my childhood had miraculously decreased in size as well! It took but a moment for me to realize that it was not the structure but I who had changed. No longer did I have the perspective of a shy and bashful young elementary school-aged girl but of an emotionally mature and secure woman.

I believe a similar analogy exists in our walk with Christ... that as we grow up in Him and view our lives through His eyes and through His Word, our view of ourselves and even our world inevitably experiences changes, and we begin to glimpse the same scene, but with mature eyes. We begin to envision, through His eyes, His divine plans for each of our lives.

Now granted, as a naive young girl, I felt woefully inadequate. And like me, perhaps some of you may have at some time in life, also vacillated between significance and inferiority, a divide possibly deepened and/or magnified by an ever-increasing entanglement in the comparison trap. Certainly, if we provide fertile ground, comparisons can often quickly become entrenched in our psyche as we, on a purely superficial level, gaze about us at others who *appear* to have it all together while we seemingly find ourselves floundering or even worse. In such instances, we may fail to genuinely celebrate the steps, however small they may be, that we have actually taken or the progress, however minute it may be, that we have actually made. In the wake of insecurity, questions such as *Who am I? Am I good enough? Why am I here? Why don't I measure up?* etc. may automatically surface. And yet, as a Christian and as a therapist, I have found an obvious, yet often overlooked question seldom asked in such cases, an underlying question that may have never been considered:

> *What was I thinking about that prompted a comparison*
> *of myself with another in the first place?*

To transparently and honestly address the above introspective question represents a fundamental first step if we are to avoid a *return* to the comparison trap, once we have successfully extricated ourselves from its grip.

Some may recall the old quip "A penny for your thoughts," but many of us may fail to realize the critical value and import of our thoughts and the significant toll that *unhealthy thoughts* often exact on us. Since our thoughts are priceless, it remains of utmost importance—actually imperative—that we intentionally question the validity of those thoughts. Why? Simply put, because our thoughts originate from our heart (or mind), the core or center of our being (Matthew 12:34; Luke 24:38, Romans 12:2).

The Bible has much to say about our thoughts. Cogently summarized in a key biblical passage familiar to many of us, King David wisely stated that as a man *thinketh in his heart, so is he* (Proverbs 23:7). In short, what we think of ourselves and how we view ourselves ultimately defines us. This, in turn, makes it critical that we intentionally guard against erroneous, small-minded thinking or, as

Moses, the writer of the book of Numbers described, a grasshopper mentality.

As Moses records in Numbers 13:32–33:

> *And they (the Israelites) brought up an evil report of the land which they had searched unto the children of Israel, saying, The land, through which we have gone to search it, is a land that eateth up the inhabitants thereof; and all the people that we saw in it are men of a great stature.*
>
> *And there we saw the giants, the sons of Anak, which come of the giants: and we were in our own sight as grasshoppers, and so we were in their sight.*

The Message Bible restates the same passage in everyday verbiage:

> *But the others said, "We can't attack those people; they're way stronger than we are." They (the ten spies) spread scary rumors among the People of Israel. They said, "We scouted out the land from one end to the other—it's a land that swallows people whole. Everybody we saw was huge. Why, we even saw the Nephilim giants (the Anak giants come from the Nephilim). Alongside them we felt like grasshoppers. And they looked down on us as if we were grasshoppers."*

The ten spies and, in turn, the children of Israel, magnified the enemy to such an extent that without having even lifted a weapon to fight their enemy, they had already accepted defeat in their minds. In a nutshell, the children of Israel had already permitted their *thoughts* and, correspondingly, their *feelings*, to define and dictate their outcome. From erroneous, self-defeated *thinking* emanated erroneous, self-defeated *feelings*.

How can we most effectively counter these false runaway thoughts that perpetuate blatant untruths and lead to false, unfounded negative emotions and feelings? Paul begins by wisely exhorting us to *change* our unhealthy thought processes. He encourages us to "let this mind be in you, which was also in Christ Jesus" (Philippians 2:5).

Unfortunately, when comparison reigns in our lives, it is easy to let our minds drift to *I wonder what he or she thinks about me?* Nonetheless, neither you nor I have any control over anyone else's thoughts and what they may or may not think about us. So rather than choosing to dwell on unproductive thinking, God shares with us in His Word *His thoughts* about us and how He feels about us. The psalmist David declares,

> *How precious also are thy thoughts unto me, O*
> *God! how great is the sum of them! If I should count*
> *them, they are more in number than the sand: when*
> *I awake, I am still with thee. (Psalm 139:17–18)*

The psalmist, David, beautifully describes the thoughts of the Awesome Creator God of the universe toward each of us, His created beings, as "precious," declaring that "great is the sum of them," and that God's thoughts of us are "more in number than the sand." David adds that when we awake, God's mind is "still" on us. In short, God is crazy about each of us. Such scripture resonates with infallible, undeniable truth. Juxtaposed against our thoughts of self-doubt and inadequacy, our Father God is cheering us on.

We can find solace as we embrace Father God's unconditional thoughts and feelings toward us. However, should we identify our own unhealthy, recurring thoughts in this process, a second step to avoid a *return* to the comparison trap is:

To specifically question and wisely consider our verbal communication,
that is, the words that proceed from our lips, and replace self-destructive
words with the infallible, unwavering truth of God's Word.

Rather than debase ourselves or others and rather than speak words antithetical to what God says about us and about others, King

Solomon wisely reminds us in Proverbs 18:21 that "death and life are in the power of the tongue: and they that love it shall eat the fruit thereof." In brief, to successfully implement step 2 and avoid a return to the comparison trap requires that we apply God's Word to our lives personally and begin to *think* and to *speak* powerful thoughts that resonate with God's truth, such as "I am accepted in the beloved" (Ephesians 1:6), "I have been brought with a price" (1 Corinthians 6:20), "I am the apple of His eye" (Zechariah 2:8), "If God be for me, who can be against me" (Romans 8:31), "I can do all things through Christ which strengtheneth me" (Philippians 4:13), etc. Such verses serve as cogent reminders to effectively circumvent our negative, self-defeating, wayward thoughts and speech.

Again, of note, to compare ourselves to others has no place in our thought life or in the words we speak. Admittedly, however, despite our best efforts, such inner or outer dialogue—often uninvited and unbridled—can still subtly weave its way into our thought processes and our verbal communication. But Almighty Father God Himself reminds us that He has "not given us a spirit of fear, but of power, of love and a *sound mind*" (2 Timothy 1:7, italics mine). In such instances, just as we change the television or radio station when we no longer like the programming, we must choose instead to deliberately change the channel in our minds from unhealthy, non-life-giving, defeated thoughts to healthy, truth-filled, God-inspiring thoughts and edifying speech.

As we purposely cast down evil thoughts and imaginations (2 Corinthians 10:5), the Apostle Paul encourages us to replace those negative thoughts we may have with thoughts of and meditation on the truths of God's infallible, powerful, awe-inspiring Word. For example, at such times, we can deliberately turn our attention and focus on the powerful instruction found in Philippians 4:8, which states, "Whatsoever things are true, whatsoever things are honest, whatsoever things are just, whatsoever things are pure, whatsoever things are lovely, whatsoever things are of good report, if there be any virtue, if there be any praise, think on these things."

Before we proceed to steps 3 and 4, which also denote two additional key strategies necessary to avoid a return to the comparison trap, let us pause briefly to further spotlight the undeniable but often overlooked correlation between step 1 (*our thoughts*) and step 2 (*our verbal communication*) and the vitally important concept of *self-talk*. (Note: For the purposes of this book, information regarding the concept of *self-talk* and any other related symptomatology is directed to the layperson and *not* to individuals with a specific mental health diagnosis or those under a psychiatrist's care.)

As a therapist, I endorse the priceless, often hidden, untapped attributes latent in *realistic self-talk*. Simply put, *self-talk* originates from our automatic thoughts (thoughts we automatically think, thoughts that involuntarily come to our minds). These automatic thoughts can be negative, false, self-defeating, etc., or, in other instances, they might be *realistic, true, reaffirming, etc.* For example, automatic thoughts, such as *She thinks she's better than me, I never do anything right,* etc., reflect uninvited, negative ideas, beliefs, etc. Conversely, automatic thoughts such as *Everyone makes mistakes, I'll do better next time,* etc., denote realistic, self-affirming thoughts, ideas, beliefs, etc. Our Lord and Savior, Jesus Christ, clearly warns us to remain alert regarding the *content* of our automatic thoughts as He notes that "out of the heart [the mind], the mouth speaks" (Matthew 12:34). In verse 37, He further warns, "For by thy words thou shalt be justified and by thy words thou shalt be condemned." Later, we are wisely admonished to cast down evil imaginations and every high thing that exalts itself against the knowledge of God (2 Corinthians 10:5). As this same passage in the Message Bible succinctly notes,

> *This world is unprincipled. It's dog-eat-dog out there! The world doesn't fight fair. But we don't live or fight our battles that way—never have and never will. The tools of our trade aren't for marketing or manipulation, but they are for demolishing that entire massively corrupt culture. We use our powerful God-tools for smashing warped philosophies, tearing down barriers erected against the truth of God, fitting every loose thought and emotion and impulse into the structure of life shaped by Christ.*

*Our tools are ready at hand for clearing the ground
of every obstruction and building lives of obedience
into maturity.* (2 Corinthians 10:3–5)

Indeed, how easy it is to harbor unhealthy and unproductive thoughts and to permit every idle, roaming, unrestrained thought to have free reign in our minds, that is, unless we intentionally discipline our minds to think God's thoughts instead. Our thoughts are so important because, in short, what we think, we may inadvertently speak, and as previously mentioned, our spoken words are powerful. So powerful, dynamic, and life-changing are our words that our Lord Jesus boldly declares in Mark 11:23: "For verily I say unto you, That whosoever shall *say* unto this mountain, Be thou removed, and be thou cast into the sea, and shall not doubt in his heart, but shall believe that those things which he *saith* shall come to pass, he shall have whatsoever he *saith*" (italics, mine).

Self-talk. Though we may never acknowledge it, at one time or another, throughout each day, we all talk to ourselves. But what do we say? A lot of what we may say about ourselves or to ourselves may or may not encompass self-defeating, self-destructive automatic thoughts. For example, our self-dialogue may include such automatic thoughts as *You can't do that, You'll mess up, Why did you do that? No one likes you, You don't look good,* etc. During disparaging inner exchanges within ourselves, it is no wonder we may not feel good about ourselves. We have been repeatedly speaking detrimental, negative, self-defeating, even condescending messages about ourselves to ourselves. Because it is often an involuntary, automatic act, self-talk can remain subtle, unnoticed, inconspicuous, etc., which is why it is imperative that we earnestly examine our thoughts and our subsequent self-talk lest we unintentionally come into agreement with the enemy of our soul.

The Bible is replete with examples of the import of our thoughts and the subsequent damaging effects of corresponding defeatist self-talk. Again, the children of Israel represent a prime example of a people who spoke their self-defeating thoughts aloud (Numbers 13:31–32). Gideon, too, shared his own negative self-concept and depiction of himself when he spoke his thoughts aloud, saying, "I am the least in my father's house" (Judges 6:15). In yet another passage, Mephibosheth, Jonathan's crippled son, openly referred to himself as a dead dog (2 Samuel 9:8).

In the field of psychotherapy, irrational beliefs are described as attitudes, ways of thinking, values, etc. that a person strongly holds as true despite objective evidence to the contrary. For example, irrational beliefs often include *must* statements and *should* statements, *all-or-nothing* statements, etc., each with an unmistakable, underlying emphasis on perfection or a perceived, optimal standard. For example, *I must be liked by everyone in my life,* is an irrational belief and is most difficult, if not impossible, to achieve.

To countermand the stronghold of the comparison trap in our self-talk, it is possible to begin to substitute an alternate *realistic* statement in place of the irrational belief we may have previously held. That's right! You and I have a choice in determining how we wish to frame our perceptions. We can abandon our irrational beliefs and remove our expectations of how it *should* be from our situation and instead invite God's Word to assume first place in our lives! In essence, we can invite God, through His Word, to have free reign in our thoughts and in our beliefs and invite His plan and His purposes to prevail in our lives!

As we now move on, the third step in our quest to avoid a return to the comparison trap, comes as we extend forgiveness. Some have aptly stated that forgiveness is *a gift that we give ourselves*, referring to the root word, *give,* in the word *forgiveness.* Let's face it! If we live long enough, someone is bound to knowingly or unknowingly offend us, hurt us, or cause us pain. And in such instances, for genuine peace to truly reign in our hearts and in our minds and so that our prayers are not hindered (Matthew 5:23–24), forgiveness is a critical ingredient that we extend to both ourselves and to others. When others have hurt us, instead of repeatedly rehearsing in our minds every ill word or criticism directed toward us or every wrongdoing seemingly perpetrated against us, one viable solution suggested to me by an anonymous minister many, many years ago is to *write* down every negative statement ever said about you or about me as well as every wrongful act or deed perpetrated against us by others. After we have done so, we reread our list of grievances once more to ensure every wrong is included and no transgression overlooked. Once our exhaustive list is complete, we tightly wad up that sheet of paper which recorded those wrongdoings and grievous actions and we throw the paper in the trash can.

Upon discarding our list, our next step is to identify scripture that clearly highlights what God says about our situation as well as what He also says about our righteousness, or right standing, in Him. Lastly, we write these scriptures down on paper and begin to intentionally meditate on the truths of God's Word. In doing this, we initiate deliberate, definitive action (physically, mentally, and spiritually), to relinquish those past wrongs and to no longer carry the added burden of unforgiveness. In no way does the completion of this exercise absolve the perpetrator of wrongdoing. However, this act of intentional forgiveness *frees* you and me from the power the perpetrator previously wielded over us when he or she consumed/occupied our every thought. Matthew 6:14–15 succinctly states, "For if ye forgive men their trespasses, your heavenly Father will also forgive you: But if ye forgive not men their trespasses, neither will your Father forgive your trespasses." In essence, it is in forgiving others that you and I effectively *take back* the power we previously gave those who may have offended us when we initially refused to release them from the grievances we held against them. Also, viewed within the backdrop of comparison, not only can we extend forgiveness to others for not meeting our expectations, expectations we felt they should have met, for hurts they may have caused, etc., but most importantly, you and I can also deliberately forgive ourselves. Perhaps it is to forgive ourselves because we did not reach our potential or, perhaps because we did not achieve an unrealistic, unsustainable goal we set for ourselves, etc.

In summary, the third step in our quest to avoid a subsequent return to the comparison trap occurs when we deliberately choose to forgive ourselves and we choose to forgive others.

In addition to monitoring our thought life, evaluating the words we speak, and forgiving ourselves and others, to most effectively avoid a return to the comparison trap also mandates an often overlooked, undervalued *fourth* step, which is:

To wisely assess when to speak and when to remain silent.

Just as our thoughts and our words are of critical import, there are also likewise *specific times or moments* when Scripture encourages us to remain silent, as when King Solomon wrote of "a time to keep silence, a time to speak" (Ecclesiastes 3:7b). At certain times, God simply admonished, "Say not" (Jeremiah 1:7). At other pivotal moments, God's people were to only speak when instructed to do so. For instance, God directed the children of Israel to march around Jericho six days but not say a word. The people of Israel obeyed and remained silent until the seventh day when, after marching around the city seven times, God instructed His people to shout in victorious unison. When they did so, the walls of Jericho fell and the Israelites "took the city" and defeated their enemy (Joshua 6:1–27).

Just as we gradually get to know a new acquaintance or learn a new facet of our job, so can we also likewise begin to intentionally identify a new, significant, interconnectedness that exists within the previously discussed, often overlooked, but critical concepts of *thoughts, verbal communication* (to include our *self-talk), forgiveness,* and *when to speak and when to remain silent.* Most importantly, we can begin to intentionally identify how each, when intricately interwoven within the fabric of our lives, can successfully thwart a *return* to the comparison trap. Once again, in brief, these four concepts:

1. To ask the critical question: *What was I thinking about that prompted a comparison of myself with another?*
2. *Verbal communication (to include self-talk), in which we specifically question and wisely consider our verbal communication, that is, the words that proceed from our lips, and intentionally replace self-destructive words with the infallible, unerring truth of God's Word.*

3. *Forgiveness, that is, we deliberately choose to forgive ourselves and to forgive others.*
4. *To wisely assess when to speak and when to remain silent.*

Notwithstanding, to successfully begin to incorporate the above steps to avoid a *return* to the comparison trap invariably necessitates time alone with God. And, in that invaluable encounter, getting to know Him on an intimate level can also correspondingly spotlight the depth of our own inner motivations and the intent of our hearts (Psalm 139:23–24).

Scripture states that Jesus sometimes retreated to a solitary place to spend time alone in prayer (Matthew 14:23; Luke 5:16). As He moved beyond the throng of the ever-present crowd, He may also compel each of us to do likewise. But, in moving past the crowd, during that precious time alone with Him, we may come to grasp and begin to realize His unique will for each of us as His children. This, in turn, further prompts us to not only give ourselves whole-heartedly to Father God but to also begin to experience significant changes in our thought life and, in turn, in our self-talk.

We cannot err if we use Jesus as our perfect example, for in the final analysis, where we came from, our roots or familial history, is not nearly as important as our destiny, that is, where we are going. But what of Jesus' familial lineage? Per Scripture, Jesus emerged from an ancestral bloodline in which one of his ancestors was a harlot, (Rahab) (Joshua 2:1; Matthew 1:5), and another, an adulterer, (David) (II Samuel 11:1–27; Matthew 1:6). Despite this, Jesus never used the conduct of those in His bloodline as a license or excuse to sin. Rather, He purposely led a sin-free life. Consequently, we, as heirs of God and joint-heirs with Christ, have no excuses to not strive to live a righteous life, for Jesus Christ remains our perfect example. However, when we fall short (and we all have, at some point), we have the assurance that Christ's blood covers every one of our sins, wrongdoings, and transgressions, for His blood cleanses us from all unrighteousness (1 John 1:7–9, Psalm 51:2, Jeremiah 33:8). It appears that God deliberately wants to ensure that we do not dwell on or even use as an excuse our family genealogy, history, status, or position or even the lack thereof as an excuse for not embracing His will and purpose for our lives. Perhaps that is why Paul, formerly named Saul, once a murderer of Christians, became the foremost writer of the New Testament (Acts 22:1–4; Philippians 3:4–10).

If making right and sometimes difficult choices ultimately dictates that you and I experience ostracism and that we are, in turn, labelled as *peculiar* or as *exceptions* to societal norms, we can remind ourselves that we are in good company, for Moses, Daniel, the disciple John, and many others were also notable *exceptions* as well! (Daniel 6:3; John 1:27; Hebrews 11:23-26; Hebrews 11:36-38).

Ah, but to be peculiar, to be the exception may not always be something we desire. In fact, it is so often easier to go *with* the flow, to go *with* the crowd. But, to achieve God's best for our lives, He requires each of us to go *beyond* the crowd. Joshua and Caleb were both examples of exceptional men who moved *beyond* the crowd (Numbers 14:37–38) as they boldly and unashamedly went against the majority and stood strong and steadfast in their beliefs. As a result, both men experienced victory and obtained *all* of God's promises for their lives (Deuteronomy 1:36, Joshua 1:3–5).

Mary, the mother of Jesus, moved *beyond* the crowd and boldly and defiantly wrestled free from entanglement in the comparison trap. Otherwise, when told by the angel that she, a virgin, would become the mother of the Savior, she would have never possessed the boldness to unabashedly respond to the angel's pronouncement that "thou shalt conceive in thy womb, and bring forth a son and shalt call his name Jesus" (Luke 1:31). Rather, it was with resolute, unwavering faith that Mary boldly declared, "Be it unto me according to thy word" (Luke 1:38).

Or had she been entangled in the comparison trap, the woman with the issue of blood never would have possessed the courage to leave her comfort zone and move *beyond* the crowd to reach out and touch the hem of Jesus' garment (Matthew 9:20). Instead, she would have cared far more about what others thought of her (after all, she was afflicted with an issue of blood and considered unclean). Yet despite her condition, she remained undeterred and pressed through the tumultuous, swelling crowd to reach Jesus, no doubt, all the while whispering, *If I can but touch the hem of his garment,* a faith-filled declaration and corresponding action which subsequently resulted in her healing.

Jesus moved *beyond* the crowd and went alone to a mountain where he was tempted after fasting for forty days. When Satan tempted Him in the wilderness, Jesus responded with "It is written" (Matthew 4:4, 7, 10). Likewise, if we are to avoid the comparison trap and its accompanying numerous pitfalls, we, too, must diligently search the Scriptures to discover what is written in God's Word. We must then purposely, intentionally apply these time-tested, unerring scriptural words and precepts of truth to our own lives. As Paul notes, "The weapons of our warfare are not carnal, but are mighty through God to the pulling down of strongholds" (2 Corinthians 10:4).

David was yet another Bible hero who went *beyond* the crowd and refused to believe the reports of others. When David stood before the giant Goliath, he had no armor. He had previously tried Saul's armor, but it did not fit (1 Samuel 17:39). There was no sword or spear in David's arsenal of weapons. Instead, he went beyond the crowd and stood boldly before Goliath in the name of the Lord (1 Samuel 17:45), armed with his own unconventional weapons, that is, his sling and a stone (1 Samuel 17:50) and his unwavering belief in the mighty, infallible God who had been with him as a young shepherd in the sheepfold (Psalm 78:70). David refused to succumb to what others dictated he should be and what weapons and armaments he should use. Nor did he take to heart their self-defeating reports regarding this enemy who threatened Israel.

Oh, for a modern-day David, Mary, Joshua, Caleb, or woman with an issue of blood. Oh, to be named among these great stalwarts of faith who refused to yield to the allure of the comparison trap and instead, as leaders, bravely dared to move *beyond* the crowd.

My Prayer

Dear Heavenly Father, my Lord and Savior God, You have set before me examples, brave forerunners who, with indomitable willpower, elected to move beyond the pale and to become all that You called each of them to be: indisputable heroes in their own right who refused to suc-cumb to entanglement in the comparison trap and who refused to submit to the status quo of their day. Instead, these men and women, despite the possible ridicule of others, dared to resolutely move beyond the crowd. They threw off the protective veil of sameness and the approval of man and, instead, dared to follow You and Your example and to ultimately please the One who called them. Can I do no less?

Equip me, Lord, to use as tools and strategies the concepts of thought, verbal communication and forgiveness that You have given to me, as well as the ability to wisely assess when to speak and when to remain silent. May I remain cognizant of my automatic thoughts and extend forgive-ness, both to myself as well as to others, so that my own prayers are not hindered. Lord, I ask that You help me to wisely choose my words and let me effectively utilize self-talk as I frequently remind myself of the iner-rant truth of Your Word and use it as both my solid foundation and as my compass on this life's journey.

When I am weak, Lord, make me strong. When I doubt, imbue me with Your faith and help me accomplish in this life the unique mission and purpose for which You have distinctly designed me and called me to fulfill. It is in the matchless, all-powerful name of Jesus Christ that I pray. Thank You, Heavenly Father, for answered prayer. Amen.

CHAPTER 6

Times and Seasons

*To everything there is a season, and a time to
every purpose under the heaven.*
—Ecclesiastes 3:1

WHILE AT WORK SEVERAL YEARS ago, a young coworker asked if she could stop by my office for a few minutes. When she arrived, she sat down and began to share with me the inner conflicts that had begun to stealthily creep into her own life. As she painstakingly shared her struggles, she transparently disclosed how she had been trying to do it all, that is, be a mother to two active, growing children, work full-time, begin a private practice, etc. By this time, her misty eyes and weary expression further highlighted the myriad of overwhelming, unresolved emotions she was experiencing. Meanwhile, her laid-bare expression of discouragement painted its own dismal picture. The silent, unrelenting demands seemed to press in upon her from all sides. No longer able to hold it all together, she brushed away the tears as they slowly coursed down her fatigued face. As if I might be her last vestige of hope, she looked at me with pleading eyes and asked me whether I, as an older woman, thought she really could "have it all." After a slight pause, I gently responded, "Yes." I resolutely told her I believed that she really could have it all—*but* I added, prefacing my statement with a critical qualifier…she might not be able to have it *all* at one time.

Never a discriminator, *time* extends its same, equal-opportunity promise to each of us. Rich, poor, Black, White, male, female…each of us, no matter our race, creed, ethnicity, sex, religion, etc., is only allotted twenty-four hours per day. And *what* we choose to do with our allotted time and *when* we choose to do it is of paramount import and, ultimately, determines the outcome. Just as true today as it was thousands of years ago when first penned, the biblical writer King Solomon thoughtfully and succinctly corroborated these realities in Ecclesiastes 3:1–8. In that passage, he began with the indisputable truth reflected in the fifteen words of verse one: "To everything, there is a season, and a time to every purpose under the heaven."

Within the comparison trap, the often overlooked, often taken for granted component of time remains a critical ingredient in any undertaking. It is within the often disregarded boundary and context of time that we may fail to accurately assess our own personal season, our own personal timeline. Entangled in the comparison trap, we briefly glimpse someone else's life or their current situation and can quickly arrive at often unwarranted, unjustified conclusions—for example, newlyweds daring to compare their tiny home or used car to the elegant home or high-end vehicle of a couple who have been married for over forty years or the unrealistic comparison that may subtly surface when a new employee compares his small cluttered, windowless cubicle to the luxurious corner office of a senior employee who has been with the company for over twenty years. Rather than embrace the principle that life is fraught with its share of "time and chance" (Ecclesiastes 9:11) for each of us, incongruous comparisons converge instead to become the faulty baseline for an erroneous and often convoluted belief system that what others have *should* be ours as well. And within this flawed and faulty schemata, prudent qualifiers, such as length of time employed, actual years worked, landmark achievements/contributions, etc., are often bypassed, overlooked, or never considered as we indiscriminately compare ourselves to others who are in a far different circumstance and/or different stage in life.

Conversely, just as we should enjoy each stage of our lives and savor each priceless moment, we must also remain alert and cognizant when the season we are in has ended and when Father God beckons us to embark upon a new, never traveled road. Sometimes this is not easy to do, but if we are to maximize each of the times and seasons of life bestowed upon us by our Heavenly Father, enter we must. Hence, it remains paramount to know *when* to move on.

One such glaring, often repeated example we may be all too familiar with occurs when a professional athlete who has experienced a successful, illustrious career decides to retire but, after a short time away from the ever-alluring bright lights, subsequently changes his mind and decides to return to his former occupation. Without doubt, the athlete may have initially recognized that it was time to move on. However, he finds the new season of retirement an unanticipated, unforeseen letdown and disappointment and totally different from the renowned, prestigious career he once enjoyed before cheering, adoring fans. Thinking that a comeback will fill the unquenchable, insatiable need and desire for affirmation from doting, devoted fans, the professional athlete, at one time at the height of his career, may soon discover reentry back into the spotlight not quite as fulfilling or rewarding as he envisioned. The sports figure may no longer possess the stamina or quick reflexes that previously catapulted him to fame. But the choice is ultimately his. The professional athlete can continue to strive to remain relevant in a season that has moved on without him, or he can gracefully exit his former occupation in life and embark upon a new calling and purpose in, heretofore, unchartered terrain. However, should he choose the latter, he may, in the process, also congruently experience unanticipated fulfillment. So it is with each of us. With each passing season of our lives, it behooves us to remain open to new, previously untapped, but nonetheless, rewarding and challenging opportunities that may await us.

For over eight years, I held a job in a dangerous and often volatile work environment. Each morning, before I walked out the door of our apartment, my dear husband would devotedly pray God's blessing of protection over me. Many, many times, I inwardly pleaded with the Lord to get me out of that hostile environment. Repeatedly, I applied to other job positions that I hoped would, in fact, result in my escape. However, for what seemed to me like an eternity, I remained there. And, amid the dangerous work conditions, God continued to keep me safe. No job opening magically materialized… until God's appointed time. In God's time, and not mine, I walked out of that precarious work environment and into a much safer work milieu.

And yet to enter a new season or new environment does not automatically guarantee a life of ease and smooth sailing, for within each new setting, new challenges also emerge. To be good at anything, to be a subject matter expert in any field, still requires time, and effort as well as that crucial component required in any worthwhile endeavor: *discipline.* Granted, God made each of us and He realizes that we are but dust (Psalm 103:14–16), and yet He is more than willing to use us, but are we willing to pay the price (2 Samuel 24:24; St. Mark 12:44)? We must be willing to be available to Him, to choose His will over our own, even when it is inconvenient and, yes, even if it requires that we suffer and endure hardship for His name's sake. While some principles inherent in the *work smarter, not harder* catchphrase are to be commended and definitely implemented, the long-term benefits of discipline and perseverance cannot be minimized.

And perhaps herein lies the most salient, indisputable, but often overlooked truth and that is, that each of us possesses the freedom to accomplish during our appointed time upon this earth what God alone has specifically designed and destined for each of us. When we purposefully, intentionally pursue God's mandate for our own individual lives, it effectively cancels out any inclination to inadvertently entangle ourselves in the comparison trap. Rather, when we are in our *sweet spot*—that is, doing what we were created to do and to be—such opportunities not only promulgate individuality but may also congruently promote levels of contentment and fulfillment not previously experienced. As we embrace the concept that it is all right to stand alone, to move *beyond* the crowd, and to be who Father God has made each of us to be, we can begin to fully revel in and appreciate God's unique design and blueprint for each of our lives.

Nonetheless, despite this life-changing revelation and regardless of our age, whether child, adolescent, or adult, there often remains a subtle, unspoken pressure to fit in, to go with the flow, to follow the latest trend, and to subsequently strive to blend in so as not to feel left behind or on the periphery. At such times, we must remind ourselves of the time-tested, tried-and-true maxim that wisely asserts that "chickens flop, but eagles soar." This insightful adage alludes to the fact that chickens flock together in groups, never going anywhere, while eagles fly alone, rising above the crowd, above the fray. And, though there is nothing inherently wrong with being fashionable, contemporary and in sync with others, when *fitting* in betrays our deepest convictions and beliefs and we ignore the apparent signpost called *truth* and choose instead to embrace the comparison trap, we betray God's purpose and design for our lives. And, in doing so, we cross an invisible line and compromise our own inherent, deepseated beliefs, values, and boundaries.

Well into the second half of my life at this juncture, I understand more fully that time is relative to God. With humans, everything may be compartmentalized into a time continuum, with definitive benchmarks—graduate from high school at eighteen, from college at twenty-two, marry at twenty-five or thirty, have two children by thirty-five, retire at sixty-five, and so forth.

But notice how *off* God's timetable is compared to man's? Without apology, He proclaimed His ways to be higher than our ways, His thoughts higher than our thoughts (Isaiah 55:8–9). Our omniscient, omnipotent God is not relegated to man's timetable or man's definition of what His creation is supposed to do or not do at certain ages. Note, for instance, how God chooses one-hundred-year old Abraham and ninety-year old Sarah to give birth to a newborn baby (Genesis 17:17). Or take the case of Moses. At eighty years of age, this meek and humble man is chosen by God to lead the children of Israel out of Egypt (Exodus 7:1–7). In yet another example, God chooses Elizabeth and Zacharias, both in their mature years, to conceive and bring forth John the Baptist, the forerunner of Jesus Christ (St. Luke 1:7-17). Anna and Simeon were both senior citizens when they finally glimpsed the promised Messiah (Luke 2:25–38).

And while God most assuredly calls the aged, on the opposite end of the spectrum, He also qualifies the young. A youth, the prophet Jeremiah reminds God that he is but a child, to which God admonishes him, "Say not, I am a child" (Jeremiah 1:7). In another instance, David, believed to be between fifteen to seventeen years of age at the time and the youngest of all his father's sons, is anointed king of Israel by the prophet Samuel (1 Samuel 16:13). And in yet another passage of Scripture, young Timothy is admonished to not let others disdain him because of his youth (1 Timothy 4:12).

In none of the aforementioned examples is age a disqualifying factor in the overall fulfillment and completion of God's purposes. As we grow older and travel life's journey and as we both celebrate the victories and weather the inequities of our lives—the good times and the bad—God's sure and steadfast promise remains the same throughout, that "...lo, I am with you alway, even unto the end of the world" (Matthew 28:20). When we walk closely with Father God throughout our lives, we develop an enduring relationship with our Savior...a relationship unique, distinct and all our own, and unlike the connection He has with any of His other children. Each of us becomes His bride and, He, our adoring bridegroom. And as His bride, we hold close to our heart His unfailing, steadfast promise that, "even to your old age I am he; and even to hoar hairs will I carry you: I have made, and I will bear; even I will carry, and will deliver you" (Isaiah 46:4).

In my adolescent years, I used to think that I was the exception—that I would *arrive* when I reached my own milestone ages, such as sixteen, eighteen, twenty-one, yes, even forty years of age. But it did not happen. I never *arrived*. Even at those landmark ages, I still experienced challenges, confronted difficult decisions, etc. Despite my temporary *successes* and despite the short-term realization of my own personal achievements/accomplishments—such as graduations, marriage, childbirth, new job positions, etc.—I never *arrived*, never reached my self-envisioned pinnacle of success. I finally realized that this is because life itself is its own journey with its own ongoing challenges.

And so, as the years have passed, I realize with greater clarity and insight that each of us is born for a special time and that God has specifically ordained each of us to fulfill our own distinct role in the fabric and tapestry of this earthly life. As Mordecai, in Esther 4:14, so insightfully reminded his niece, Queen Esther, with wise words that likewise reverberate for our own lives, it is "for such a time as this" that each of us is here. Most assuredly, you and I could have been born at any other time in history (that is, in the 1300s, the 1800s, etc.), but instead, we were born in the twentieth or twenty-first century—for this time and for this season.

So why pursue an ordinary existence in which we compare ourselves to others who must also choose whether or not they will live out their own specific, God-ordained, God-directed destiny? Why purposely seek to mimic, imitate, or live in the shadow of another? And yet the comparison trap can ever so subtly beckon us to do just that! And that is to follow the path laid out for others rather than embrace the unique, individualized, one-of-a-kind blueprint God has carefully, meticulously carved out for each of us as His children. Could it be that God simply wants us to adhere to the specific plan and purpose He has so carefully designed for each of us? And yes, in short, to answer that call is to simply be faithful even in what we ourselves may label as mundane and, yes, again to remain faithful, even if our sphere is small and even if, in the eyes of others, our destiny may appear insignificant, even miniscule. Scripture, however, clearly exhorts that we despise not the day of small beginnings (Zechariah 4:10), for it is the continual, day-to-day building upon a sure but steady and firm foundation that engenders great rewards and an immeasurable harvest. David began as a shepherd boy but eventually reigned as king of Israel (2 Samuel 7:8–13).

Undoubtedly, each of us is at a different time or season in our lives. It may sound ludicrous, but have you ever considered why two-year-old children aren't permitted to get their driver's licenses or why seventy-year-old men don't try out for an NFL team? Though such questioning, in and of itself, sounds bizarre, preposterous or nonsensical at best, it clearly illustrates the importance of recognizing distinct times and seasons in our lives.

As a therapist, I meet with individuals of various ages who are in different seasons of their lives. At times, I have met with an older individual who laments no longer being able to perform more demanding activities—such as jogging, exercising, even driving, etc., activities that may have once given that individual immense pleasure, fulfillment, and independence. To forever say farewell to an activity that played such a significant role in that individual's life can cause unspeakable angst and even lead to depression. What can be done in such a case? Perhaps a salient starting point can be to ensure that the person does *not* assimilate society's definition of him based on his age. Rather, it is imperative that the individual begins to search for and embrace the unique gifts, talents, and abilities that still reside within him in his current season of life.

Next, as God asked the eighty-year-old Moses, it is prudent that we each also similarly ask ourselves: *what do you have in your hand* (Exodus 4:2)? The response to such a thought-provoking question can be the launching pad to previously overlooked and perhaps untapped potential never considered or explored. Can you and I begin to do something right now with what we currently have in our hands? When the widow's two sons were to soon be taken as bondmen because their mother could not pay her family's debt, Elijah, the prophet, asked a similarly poignant question: "Tell me, what hast thou in the house?" (2 Kings 4:2). Rather than comparing ourselves with others, can we instead examine what we are doing with what we currently have within our grasp? To do so may unleash powerful, untapped, hidden treasures lying dormant within each of us in this previously unexplored season of our lives.

But what if we have permitted our chronological age or current societal expectations to define us or, better yet, what if we are no longer physically capable of those activities that once gave us such joy and fulfillment? Can we begin to actually embrace the season we are in, discover alternate outlets, and explore new, never-before-tried, never considered options? I pose this question again because the response warrants additional scrutiny! The willingness to do something we've never done before could be the segue to unexplored opportunities we have never considered or that we assumed were out of reach, but could potentially result in never-tried open doors.

Granted, as I get older, I too realize the finality of this temporal life. Not as young as I once was, I have begun to consider the extent of the legacy and contributions my husband and I wish to leave our adult children, our grandchildren, and, ultimately, the world. For like you, we too have a choice. We can take what is in our hand and, like the wise stewards, multiply and cultivate our gifts for the benefit of God's kingdom and future generations, or we can be like the unwise steward who simply buried his talent (Matthew 25:24–25).

It is essential, therefore, that we earnestly and fervently pray (James 5:16) and ask God to help us recognize the specific times and seasons in our lives, and most importantly, that we ask our Heavenly Father for cogent ways we can most effectively serve and glorify Him in new, previously unexplored areas of our lives. To do so will circumvent any propensity to compare ourselves to others or to march to the beat of another's drum. Most importantly, this also provides a distinct, God-ordained opportunity for each of us to fully embrace our own God-given uniqueness.

Additionally, with the passage of time, it remains critical for each of us to treasure each and every moment that God has allotted to us, even when circumstances may prove less than optimal. As he has gotten older, my dad often shakes his head in wonderment just about every time the family gets together or I visit him and my mom. In amazement, Dad will shake his head and remark, "You know, the time passes so fast. The time passes so fast!" And Dad is so right!

The King James Bible records "Now it came to pass" or one of its related derivatives at least 452 times (https://bibleteacher. org/2017/12/17/it-came-to-pass/). Such words evoke their own pronouncement because for none of us did time come to stay. James, believed to be the brother of Jesus, explicitly asks the reader in James 4:14, "For what is your life? It is even a vapour, that appeareth for a little time, and then vanisheth away." In short, for each of us, our lives will "come to pass." However, it is up to each of us how we most expeditiously utilize our lives and the brief time we have each been given on this earth. Will we squander it, or will we redeem it (Ephesians 5:16)? Will we use it to hide and bury our talents, as referenced earlier in Matthew 25:24–25, or will we multiply our talents for the glory of God and for His kingdom (Matthew 25:21–23)? Assuredly, there are no guarantees in life. However, one thing is certain. Whatever state—that is, situation, circumstance, moment in time, etc.—in which we find ourselves, it too, will come to pass.

The concept of time itself can be compartmentalized into seasons. Take for instance the ant, lauded in Proverbs 6:6 and Proverbs 30:25, who busily stores up his food for the approaching winter season. Like the ant, it behooves us to also wisely prepare and make provision as much as we possibly can in all facets of our lives, that is, spiritually, financially, physically, emotionally, etc. In the natural, just because we may have a great paying job today does not mean it will be there tomorrow, which wisely necessitates a prudent savings/investment plan. Likewise, from a spiritual perspective, in the current season in which we find ourselves, we must build our house not upon sand (Matthew 7:24–27), but upon a solid, spiritual foundation for, in so doing, we are prepared when the strong winds of adversity assail us. In addition, as we willingly take a risk and explore new venues, Father God reassures us in His Word, "Fear thou not; for I am with thee: be not dismayed; for I am thy God: I will strengthen thee; yea, I will help thee; yea, I will uphold thee with the right hand of my righteousness" (Isaiah 41:10). All the while, throughout life's storms and its many ups and downs, we keep before us a steadfast, unwavering faith in our Heavenly Father's promise: "My presence shall go with thee" (Exodus 33:14). God's promises comfort us and light our pathway regardless of the season in which we find ourselves. Furthermore, to encourage us along our journey, the psalmist David implores our Heavenly Father to "teach us to number our days, that we may apply our hearts unto wisdom" (Psalm 90:12).

To effectively recognize the times and seasons within the framework of comparison also conversely mandates that we remain leery of *complacency*, a subtle but often insidious, self-defeating mindset in which one becomes satisfied with one's achievement or station in life and no longer tries to achieve more or reach further. An additional, often-overlooked but similar juxtaposition—of which we must likewise remain equally wary—is the inclination to *simply settle*, that is, to settle for less than God's best when God has called us to so much more. When we are in step with God's plan for our lives, we recognize and instinctively move as He moves (Exodus 13:21–22).

As avid proponents of motivation, drive, and perseverance in our pursuit of God's best for our lives, we must remain hypervigilant when their diametrically opposed counterparts—*complacency* and the propensity to *simply settle*—attempt to deter us from God's best for us. Likewise assuming that bad times will last always is diametrically opposed to Father God's promise to each of us that "weeping may endure for a night, but joy cometh in the morning" (Psalm 30:5). We must remind ourselves as we press forward that circumstances and situations—whether good or bad—usually only last for a specific time and season.

To shake us out of any self-imposed lethargy, complacency, or a tendency to compare, the questions we may ultimately need to ask or discern in such instances are the following: *What is God's will in this matter? What is God's will for my situation?* Additionally, *is what I propose to do, to be, or to have, Father God's best for my life in this current time and season?*

Doubtless, our God sometimes delights in the nontraditional, the unexplainable, and even what is seemingly irrational to our human mind and senses. While our finite timeframe confines us to twenty-four hours a day, seven days a week, fifty-two weeks a year, we can take solace in God's Word "that one day is with the Lord as a thousand years, and a thousand years as one day" (2 Peter 3:8). He is also "mindful that we are but dust" (Psalms 103:14–16).

Psalm 90:10 numbers man's brief travail on earth at threescore and ten years and, if by reason of strength and labor, four score years. And yet within that brief expanse of time and within the backdrop of eternity, the allure of comparison will repeatedly raise its ugly head and continue to play an insidious, uninvited role in our lives, if we let it. As a teenager, do you even remember that CD you were just dying to have or that bomb outfit you just couldn't do without? How about that teen movie idol or heartthrob you spent every waking hour thinking about? Where is that CD, that outfit, and that singing sensation now? For many, those *must-have* items, now relegated to the attic or basement, are no longer touted as valuable. The teen idols have lost their allure, charisma, even their looks. With repeated washings, the chic outfit we once felt we had to have, has begun to fade in color, to bust at the seams, the buttons to fall off, or worse yet, our friends don't wear that style because it is no longer fashionable or trendy. Or in our now *instant* society, rather than wait for what we want, we want everything right now. In such a setting, if we are not disciplined, we can begin to abruptly dismiss the time-honored principles inherent in deferred gratification. Instead, we become easily frustrated when we must wait extra moments in the checkout line at the grocery store or in bumper-to-bumper rush hour traffic. Instead of basking in the moment, relishing uniqueness and simplicity, we instinctively rush off to the next big event, never pausing to embrace the present.

And just why are the times and the seasons of our lives so transient? Why don't these things upon which we set our affections last? In brief, it is because this is not our permanent home. As previously mentioned earlier in this chapter, on this side of eternity, life is but "a vapor, that appeareth for a little time, and then vanisheth away" (James 4:14). As the psalmist David so aptly entreats God in Psalms 39:4–5,

> *Lord, make me to know mine end, and the measure of my days, what it is; that I may know how frail I am.*
> *Behold, thou hast made my days as a hand breadth; and mine age is as nothing before thee; verily every man at his best state is altogether vanity. Selah.*

Prayer

Lord, help me to redeem the time You have given to me. Teach me to number my days, that I may apply my heart to wisdom (Psalm 90:12). Help me to realize that it is futile and unproductive to compare myself to others and to make them my unrealistic, unattainable, and unsustainable yardstick. Instead, I ask that You establish the work of my hands (Psalm 90:17) and help me to glorify You throughout the times and seasons of my life.

Help me not grow weary in well-doing and help me to remember that I ultimately work for only one—for You and You alone. You, Father God, are my reward and the lifter of my head (Psalm 3:3). Help me to make every moment of every day of my life count for You, and help me to never accept the insidious lie that I compare myself with others who are anointed by You to run a different race than mine. Rather, let me run the distinct race that You have set before me. Thank You for the wisdom to use this gift of time and this season in which You have placed me for Your glory. In the priceless, matchless name of Jesus Christ, I pray. Amen.

CHAPTER 7

Decisions

*Multitudes, multitudes in the valley of decision: for the
day of the Lord is near in the valley of decision.*
                                        —Joel 3:14

EVER HEARD THE OFT-REPEATED STATEMENT, "He looks just like his father"? Without doubt, my husband would be highly upset, and I would too, if our adult sons bore no family resemblance to us or to other family members. However, our sons possess distinct traits and features of their father. And so it is with our Heavenly Father. He wants His children to resemble Him, that is, display His mannerisms, speak His words, think His thoughts, etc.

Just as I can quickly identify certain familiar traits of my husband in our sons, my thoughts invariably turn to my own relationship with God. Can others who observe my speech and actions readily identify me as my Heavenly Father's daughter, or would they be hard-pressed to note any resemblance or identifying characteristics of Father God in me at all? I believe that the closer I walk with Father God, the more of His character and His perspective I assimilate and take on as my own.

Decisions, time, comparison—three totally different, disparate concepts, and yet when they converge, they can significantly determine or alter the course of our lives. Decisions can often play a crucial and even life-changing role when placed within the framework

77

of time on one end of the spectrum and, contrariwise, an incessant, seemingly never-ending battle with comparison at the other end. As a result, the quality of each decision is impacted, which, in turn, exacts its own unforeseen toll and outcome. As we travel this journey of life, what we choose to do or not do and who we choose to be or not be, eventually represents the final determinant in whether we assume the role of victor or victim in our own ongoing struggle to avoid comparison and subsequent entanglement in the comparison trap. Even when we decide *not* to make a decision, we are making a decision…even if it is a decision *not* to choose.

Without question, the most important life's decision we will ever make is whether we will accept Jesus Christ as our Lord and Savior and whether we will serve Him. In 1 Kings 18:21, Elijah boldly confronted the people of Israel with a piercing question: "How long halt ye between two opinions? If the Lord be God, follow him: but if Baal, then follow him." Previously, in Joshua 24:15, Joshua challenged the Israelites: "Choose you this day whom ye will serve." Then, in an unwavering response to his own courageous edict, Joshua fearlessly declared, "As for me and my house, we will serve the Lord."

While life's most important question never changes, what of our small, not-so-noticeable decisions? Do they matter? Often overlooked are the benefits of ignoring the false allure of comparison and what others may say/do and, instead, purposefully pointing a penetrating spotlight on the long-term ramifications that wise, prudent decisions can engender. Notably, it is in the small, often minimized details—that is, the daily fifteen-minute exercise program, the daily thirty-minute quiet prayer and Bible reading time, the repetitive sharing of truths with our children, the continual "eating right" and making wise nutritional choices, etc.—that, in turn, result in long term, consistent success and tangible benefits for the disciplined individual who maintains a steady, undeterred, determined mindset and regimen. Although you and I may not see any substantive change as we perform these daily tasks, one day—it may be ten, twenty, or even thirty years from now—we may see a harvest from the good seed we have diligently planted, watered, and tilled.

Sometimes it may be hard to comprehend, but the choices we make, what we choose to do, and choose *not* to do, not only affect us but may have long-lasting positive or negative consequences and ramifications for those closest to us.

The Bible poignantly recounts such an example in both the story of Abraham and the story of Achan in the Bible. Scripture records that Abraham walked with God, and both he and his children were blessed. In Genesis 22:18, the angel of God tells Abraham, "And in thy seed shall all the nations of the earth be blessed because thou hast obeyed my voice."

On the other hand, Achan, inextricably mired in covetousness, had secretly taken that which did not belong to him. This not only led to his own demise but also led to the destruction of his entire family lineage as Joshua 7:20–21, 24–25 clearly records,

> *And Achan answered Joshua, and said, Indeed I have sinned against the Lord God of Israel. (Joshua 7:20)*

> *When I saw among the spoils a goodly Babylonish garment, and two hundred shekels of silver, and a wedge of gold of fifty shekels weight, then I coveted them, and took them. (Joshua 7:21)*

> *And Joshua and all Israel with him, took Achan the son of Zerah, and the silver, and the garment, and the wedge of gold, and his sons, and his daughters, and his oxen, and his asses, and his sheep, and his tent, and all that he had: and they brought them unto the valley of Achor. (Joshua 7:24)*

> *And Joshua said, Why hast thou troubled us? the Lord shall trouble thee this day. And all Israel stoned him with stones, and burned them with fire, after they had stoned them with stones. (Joshua 7:25)*

The above accounts illustrate the diametrically opposed decisions and subsequent outcomes of Abraham and Achan, two very different men. Their divergent decisions clearly delineate the far-reaching mandate upon each of us, not only for ourselves, but for the sake of our children, our families, and others to walk above *reproach* and to ensure that neither comparison nor covetousness be named among us. A word not normally used in everyday conversation, *Webster's* dictionary defines *reproach* as "a cause or occasion of blame, discredit or disgrace." We are mandated to walk above reproach, that is, *above* blame, discredit, or disgrace.

In Joshua 1:8, the author unapologetically challenges God's people, the Israelites, to resolute, decisive action as he admonishes "This Book of the Law shall not depart out of thy mouth, but thou shalt meditate therein day and night, that thou mayest observe to do according to all that is written therein." Joshua adds that if this command is adhered to, it will be followed by irrefutable results…"for then thou shalt make thy way prosperous, and then thou shalt have good success."

In short, our decisions and our choices are simply byproducts of our intrinsic values. We may spend countless years and expend thousands upon thousands of man-hours to acquire the earnings on our jobs necessary to purchase material things, but at what cost? When pursued in excess, those actions may ultimately be to the detriment of our relationship with those we most value. For each of us, the question becomes, what do we most value, prize, treasure? It has been said that at the end of our lives, we will not wish that we had spent more time on our jobs but, rather, that we spent more time with those we most love and cherish.

But what of our ill-considered, ill-advised decisions? I may not see the results of my unwise decisions and impulsive choices—for example, instances of unforgiveness, hurtful words, negative lifestyle, etc.—until one day I awaken to find myself reaping the consequences of those actions, terse words and negative behaviors. Perhaps we may derive some momentary degree of satisfaction or pleasure, but what of the unforeseen long-term adverse results of our poor decisions? Certainly, the decisions are each of ours to make, for each of us plays an integral role in our own life story. As we reflect on our own history (past), God gives us the opportunity, via the decisions we make, to pen both our present and our future destiny. The path we choose and the subsequent results of those decisions fall squarely at our own feet. As Paul the apostle wisely attests, "Be not deceived; God is not mocked: for whatsoever a man soweth, that shall he also reap" (Galatians 6:7).

And yet, just as our wrong decisions can adversely affect us and our loved ones so, too, can the deliberate, intentional right decisions we make result in a blessing and a bountiful harvest in both our lives and in the lives of our family members. Notice the narrative of Rahab, for instance. The book of Joshua records that because Rahab risked her own safety and dared to hide the spies, Joshua "saved Rahab the harlot alive, and her father's household, and all that she had; and she dwelleth in Israel even unto this day; because she hid the messengers, which Joshua sent to spy out Jericho" (Joshua 6:25).

So it is with those of us who have been engrafted into God's holy family through our acceptance of Jesus Christ as our personal Savior. As sons and daughters of Father God, no longer do we make decisions antithetical to our "royal priesthood" (1 Peter 2:9). Rather, by faith, we walk worthy of the "vocation" (Ephesians 4:1) to which we have each been called, in particular, reminding ourselves that "every good gift and every perfect gift is from above, and cometh down from the Father of lights, with whom is no variableness, neither shadow of turning" (James 1:17). And since all our gifts emanate from the munificent hand of our Heavenly Father, our Creator God, we have no reason to glory. After all, are we not stewards of what God has so generously bestowed upon us all? And what does the role of a steward or a manager require? In response, Paul notes in 1 Corinthians 4:2, "Moreover, it is required in stewards that a man is found faithful."

Hence, no matter the extent of our gifts, skills, talents or abilities, our role is not to boast, except in God (1 Corinthians 1:31) and to be faithful. Psalms 44:8 declares, "In God, we boast all the day long, and praise thy name forever. Selah." In short, our mandate is clear and succinct, and that is, to simply be good stewards of what we have been given. When we make our boast in God, the need to compare ourselves with others quickly vanishes.

History is behind us, seen in our rearview mirror, while our future and our destiny beckon. We are all too familiar that the clichés (such as fifteen minutes of fame, a fading star, a has-been), as well as the movie stars, celebrities, legends, etc., come and go, but such is never the case with God. With Him, we never come and go. No matter our wrong decisions, our careless mistakes, we are never a *has-been* with Father God. Rather, He "hath raised us up together and made us sit together in heavenly places in Christ Jesus" (Ephesians 2:6). No matter if we are at our lowest point, God does not forget us or abandon us. While dying on the cross, the thief hanging next to Jesus, asked our Lord and Savior to remember him when Jesus came into His kingdom. With deep love and compassion, Jesus responded, "Verily I say unto thee, this day shalt thou be with me in paradise" (Luke 23: 42–43).

As a result, like the thief on the cross, we, too, also have this most blessed assurance that, even our unwise, misguided decisions of the past do not determine our final destiny. In fact, we dare not permit our past history to dictate our present and future possibilities, for in doing so, we do both ourselves and the redemptive act of our Lord and Savior, Jesus Christ, a disservice. Rather, "forgetting those things which are behind, and reaching forth unto those things which are before," (you and) I press toward the mark for the prize of the high calling of God in Christ Jesus" (Philippians 3:13–14).

The Bible further admonishes us that, whatever we do, we are to "do it heartily, as to the Lord and not unto men" (Colossians 3:23). We are reminded that our "expectation [which includes any subsequent rewards/results] is from God" (Psalm 62:5). And because God is just, He will give to each of us our reward.

When viewed through the lens of comparison, however, our fellow man may or may not reward or compensate us for our achievements/accomplishments, or, for that matter, even acknowledge or notice our actions/efforts. Again, however, our Abba, Father, is our rewarder, and He alone is faithful to remember our "labor of love" (1 Thessalonians 1:3, Hebrews 6:10). Eventually, though, we must each ask ourselves what compels us to do what we do and to make the decisions that we make?

And why is it so critical to be single in eye, unwavering, not double-minded as James warns in James 1:6–8? Simply put, when our allegiance is to so many others—that is, to our spouse, parents, children, siblings, friends, supervisor, employees, etc.—our hearts, our minds, our complete devotion, can never be fully His. Thus, we will always have divided loyalties, always have a divided heart. And instead of wanting to totally please Christ, we will want to please those we hold in high esteem, those whose positive affirmations we covet.

As with each pass/fail mark in school that we garner, life too offers its own set of tests/exams. And eventually, it is up to each of us to pass the tests that this life throws at us. My husband is fond of saying, "If you don't pass life's test the first time, be sure that you will have to take the make-up exam." The children of Israel experienced many failed mountain crossings/make-up exams. In fact, they had so many failed mountain crossings/make-up exams that the Lord spoke to them and said, "Ye have dwelt long enough in this mount. Turn you and take your journey" (Deuteronomy 1:6–7). And again, in Deuteronomy 2:3, God spoke unto Moses, saying, "Ye have compassed this mountain long enough: turn you northward."

If you and I become embroiled in needless, worthless comparisons, and we blindly embrace what others say about us as our own definition of ourselves, we inevitably sell ourselves short and negate God's precious truths. Equipped with incomplete versions of who we really are, we never break free of the chains of comparison. Think of it! In our own self-inflicted bondage, we never realize our own God-given, unique greatness or the true freedom bestowed upon us by our Creator God to be the best, to be an original, a masterpiece, a one of a kind.

So when is enough, enough? How much must we acquire to reach that pinnacle, that place, where we one day experience enduring contentment and satisfaction? How much must we acquire to finally arrive at that place in God where who we are in Him is, in itself, enough? Is it possible to simply be the very best we can be, to do so with all our might, as unto the Lord and then to leave the results to God?

Or must we succumb to comparison or, even worse, to instances of groupthink, in which our thoughts are dictated by the prevalent mindset of the culture about us? If we are to ever move beyond the crowd and achieve our uniqueness as God's priceless jewel, our continual goal must be to *fight the good fight* (2 Timothy 4:7) deep within our minds and embrace God's Word about us and not society's definition of us. Whether we plan to or not, each day we write another page of our life's history. What must you do, what must I do, to make our own distinct and lasting legacy, a legacy unimpeded by what others think, say, or do, a legacy that effectively breaks free from the stifling tentacles of comparison with others, to become all that God made each of us to be?

Prayer

Lord, as I make life decisions each day, free me from the comparison trap, from its lies, deceptions, and falsehoods. Help me to disdain comparison with others. Instead, help me to become intentional, focused, and wholly dedicated in my devotion to You. Help me to guard what I think, say and do. Let me not succumb to the negative influence of others nor fall victim to what others may say or do if it is not corroborated by the truth found in Your Word. For in erroneously doing so, I unintentionally set the stage for the reality I may subsequently experience.

Rather, Father God, like Jabez, I ask that You increase my capacity to pray bigger and believe bigger and begin to conceive what I might truly accomplish for You (1 Chronicles 4:9–10). Increase my capacity to not only think bigger but to see myself doing more, gaining more, being more, and conquering new territory for You, my Lord and Savior.

Let me steadfastly run the race that You have set before me. And on that great and final day when time shall be no more, may I stand before You and hear You say, "Well done, good and faithful servant; you have been faithful over a few things, I will make you ruler over much" (Matthew 25:23). Father God, let my life and all I am, from this moment forth, be to the glory of Your majestic and holy name, both now and forever! For it is in the exalted, all-powerful name of Our Lord and Savior, Jesus Christ, I pray. Amen.

CHAPTER 8

Launch Out into the Deep

*Now when he had left speaking he said unto Simon, "Launch
out into the deep, and let down your nets for a draught."*
—Luke 5:4

TO PROTECT OUR HOME COMPUTERS from viruses, my husband installed an antivirus software program on each of our computers. Now, periodically, as I busily complete a project or work assignment, a small sidebar in the right-hand bottom corner of my computer screen will silently appear—a reminder that the software program is consistently at work, shielding my computer from unwanted cyber intruders. Similarly, within the spiritual realm, the Holy Spirit of God, our Comforter and Guide, also acts as our protective, filtering agent. The Holy Spirit is constantly at work, not only to comfort us but to also warn us and guide us into all truth so that we do not fall prey to the often subtle yet dangerous and devious attacks of the enemy. And yet despite the work of the Holy Spirit, God also calls each of us to be responsible, to do our part, and to "be sober, be vigilant; because your adversary the devil, as a roaring lion, walketh about, seeking whom he may devour" (1 Peter 5:8). So, no matter our status in life—that is, our claim to fame or to anonymity, our burgeoning bank account, or our complete lack of finances, from the beggar in the street to the president in the White House—each is equal in the eyes of our Father God. And Revelation 20:12 clearly forewarns that each of us—the "small and great"—will one day stand before Him.

Once, while driving my car in the dark of night I, without warning, glimpsed an indistinguishable figure walking near the side of the road. I quickly swerved in time and narrowly missed hitting the young man attired in all dark clothing. Thank God! With the same razor-edge intensity and keen awareness in which God blessed me to see that previously unobtrusive pedestrian suddenly appear in my vision, so must each of us, with equally keen, intentional awareness, seek to hear our Lord's wisdom, direction, and guidance in our everyday lives.

And yet there are times when our sight and what we *see* before us can actually paralyze us or thwart any attempts on our part to action and may instead lead us to inaction and to failure. Unhealthy thoughts can as well. For instance, thoughts regarding inferiority, such as the grasshopper mentality of the children of Israel (previously discussed in chapter 5 of this book), warrant further consideration. Not only was the *thinking* of the Israelites negatively impacted in this instance but their *sight* and what the children of Israel were *seeing* also impacted their ability to *believe* God for victory.

In short, what we *see* before us with our naked eye can impede or even diminish our faith to believe God for victory in the spiritual realm. And, instead, what we see before us engenders fear. Once again, as recorded in Numbers, the 13th chapter, 13:30–33,

> *And Caleb stilled the people before Moses, and said, Let us go up at once and possess it; for we are well able to overcome it. But the men that went up with him said, We be not able to go up against the people; for they are stronger than we… The land through which we have gone to search it, is a land that eateth up the inhabitants thereof; and all the people that we saw are men of a great stature. And there we saw the giants, the sons of Anak…we were in our own sight as grasshoppers and so we were in their sight.*

Of the twelve men who spied out the enemy land, only Caleb and Joshua exhibited courage, conviction, and unerring faith in both their words and in their corresponding actions (Numbers 13:30). Despite what Caleb and Joshua *saw,* they moved forward with courage and unerring faith.

In times of challenge and uncertainty, when we cannot *see* our way clearly, we must lean assuredly and without wavering on God's Word alone. As Caleb and Joshua boldly declared,

> *If the Lord delight in us, then he will bring us*
> *into this land and give it us; a land which floweth*
> *with milk and honey.* (Numbers 14:8)

Like Caleb and Joshua, when we know that God has more for us, patience and persistence must remain our steadfast mantra and our consistent battle cry. Jacob is yet another example of a giant in the faith who persisted despite difficulty. The book of Genesis recounts that he wrestled with an angel throughout the night to the breaking of the next day:

> *And he (the angel) said, Let me go, for the day*
> *breaketh. And he (Jacob) said, I will not let thee go,*
> *except thou bless me. And he said unto him, What*
> *is thy name? And he said, Jacob. And he said, Thy*
> *name shall be called no more Jacob, but Israel: for as*
> *a prince hast thou power with God and with men,*
> *and hast prevailed.* (Genesis 32:26–28)

In yet another example, Nehemiah, in rebuilding the wall, refused to give up or to give in, for though opposition came, he and the men who followed him, continued to build.

> *Everyone with one of his hands wrought in the*
> *work, and with the other hand held a weapon...*
> *For the builders, everyone had his sword girded by*
> *his side, and so builded.* (Nehemiah 4:17b–18)

The previous scriptural passage indicates that pursuing our purpose, our mission, our God-given goals in this life may not be easy. In fact, our path may be fraught with danger, with adversity, with struggle, and with pain. Despite this, like the Jewish leader, Nehemiah, who held a weapon in one hand and a work utensil in another, we, too, continue to work, to fight, to never give up. Instead, we steadfastly persevere and march forward.

In yet another poignant example of persistence in the face of adversity, Joshua admonishes the children of Israel to press forward:

> *And Joshua said unto the children of Israel,*
> *How long are ye slack to go to possess the land,*
> *which the Lord God of your fathers hath given you?*
> *(Joshua 18:3)*

Certainly, there are some exceptions in which little to no effort is required to pursue or obtain our goals. For instance, in 2 Chronicles 20:17, God specifically instructed the children of Israel, "Ye shall not need to fight in this battle; set yourselves, stand ye still, and see the salvation of the Lord with you." But even in this instance, the people of Israel saw victory *only* when they specifically began to *praise God Almighty,* as noted in the below passage:

> *And when they began to sing and to praise,*
> *the Lord set ambushments against the children of*
> *Ammon, Moab, and mount Seir, which were come*
> *against Judah, and they were smitten.* (2 Chronicles
> 20:22)

Again, only as they began to sing and give praise to God did the children of Israel see and experience victory!

As a young girl, I remember hearing a preacher insightfully remark that two-thirds of God's name is comprised of the word "Go," which clearly denotes action. Jesus Himself exhorted His disciples to go, to "launch out into the deep" (Luke 5:4). For Noah to leave the safety of the Ark he had built, he had to risk and go (Genesis

8:15–17). Abraham had to leave a familiar land and venture into the unknown (Genesis 11:26–32). Launching out into the deep may not just entail a physical transition or leaving a particular area. Rather, it may also entail praising our God in the face of adversity, taking a bold action totally out of our comfort zone, etc.

And yet as we depart the safety of the shore, and we launch out into the deep, our omniscient, omnipresent Father God is right there, lovingly reassuring us, "I, even I, am he that comforteth you" (Isaiah 51:12).

So perhaps with trepidation and even with some degree of apprehension, we, like Noah and Abraham before us, launch out into our own heretofore unexplored deep. In doing so, it is not for comparison's sake—that is, to *outdo*, to *out be*, or to imitate someone else—that we journey forth. Rather, we launch out into the deep because we, like Peter, remain intent on following our Lord's call (Matthew 14:28–29). And as staunch followers of our Lord and Savior, Jesus Christ, we refuse to dawdle. Rather, we remain steadfastly focused, intent to closely follow and adhere to His distinct design and plan for our individual lives.

As you and I dare to launch out into the deep, can we begin to highlight our own gifts? Not someone else's, but our own! Scripture declares that "every good gift and every perfect gift is from above and cometh down from the Father of lights, with whom is no variableness, neither shadow of turning" (James 1:17). At birth, God had already deposited His gifts into each of us (Jeremiah 1:5). However, it remains essential for each of us to "stir up" those gifts (2 Timothy 1:6), to develop those gifts, and to use them for *His* Glory; for "none of us have whereof to glory" (Romans 4:2) because all we have and possess comes from Him.

Without doubt, to successfully reign in this life, we must appropriate the full armor of God (Ephesians 6:10–18). But our journey does not end there! We must then be willing to move away from the safety of the shore and risk launching out in to the deep. And yet even as we do so, it is prudent to frequently recall past victories we have experienced as a direct result of Father God's help and intervention, perhaps victories in which we may have previously fought some of life's toughest battles. All the while, we encourage ourselves that even in our current struggles, "Faithful is he that calleth you, who also will do it" (1 Thessalonians 5:24).

In conclusion, it is during those past, difficult, perhaps even harrowing times, that we can remind ourselves that we were never alone but that our Father God was always at the helm, always consistently and repeatedly showing Himself faithful and true then as He continues to do today and will do in the future. Why? Because for time immemorial, He will never change. He is "the same yesterday, and today, and forever" (Hebrews 13:8) and He is Jesus Christ, "my rock, and my fortress, and my deliverer; my God, my strength, in whom I will trust; my buckler, and the horn of my salvation, and my high tower" (Psalm 18:2).

Prayer

Dearest Father God, You did not make a mistake when You made me. Jeremiah 1:5 proclaims that before You formed me in the belly and before I came out of my mother's womb, You knew me and ordained me. And within me, You bestowed magnificent gifts exclusive to Your blueprint for my life. Lord, in my quest to give You glory and to honor You with my life and in in my ardent refusal to compare myself to others, let me also congruently strive to launch out in to the deep. Let me strive to become all that You have destined for me, following Your own unique master plan for my life. I realize I have nothing of which to boast, for every gift and calling comes from You (James 1:17, Romans 11:29). But, Lord, let me earnestly stir up and cultivate Your gifts within me. And, having done so, let me always use those gifts to Your glory and lay them at Your feet as a praise offering to You, the One who gave them to me.

To move beyond the throes of comparison, I must, like Peter, be willing to lose sight of the familiar and the comfortable. Most of all, to walk on the water with You, my Lord, my Savior, my dearest Friend, I must lose sight of the shore. Thank You for the faith to do so! It is in the magnificent Name of Jesus Christ I pray. Amen.

CHAPTER 9

Battle to Victory

And ye are complete in him…

—Colossians 2:10a

IT WAS A TYPICAL HOT and humid summer day in Texas. My husband and I drove the short distance to the grocery store, made our purchases, and had just returned to our van. It was then that we both saw it for the first time. The tint of the sun on the dashboard drew our attention to the previously never-before-seen letters "O/D" hidden unobtrusively in the dashboard.

For six years, we had owned our van. And, for six years, we'd had hidden, untapped power via our van's overdrive (O/D), but we never knew we possessed it because we never intensely studied the owner's manual.

So it is in our relationship with the Lord. Unless we read the owner's manual—in this instance, God's Word, the Holy Bible— we will never truly begin to experience His divine master plan or unearth His fathomless power or the life-giving promises that our Heavenly Father has for each of us.

In addition to strategies discussed earlier in this book targeted to help us *break free* and *stay free* from the grip of comparison, we will never conceivably reach overdrive, that is, our full potential in life, and become all that God has destined us to be if we do not remain vigilant and recognize the underlying subtleties inherent within the

91

comparison trap. The indisputable mark of true spiritual maturity is when you and I choose to intentionally ward off the tendency to compare ourselves to others. And, instead, we deliberately choose to run, with Christ at the helm, our own individual race, a race in which we strive to become God's masterpiece, exclusively designed and fashioned by Creator God Himself. As 1 Corinthians 9:24–25 so aptly states,

> *Know ye not that they which run in a race run all, but one receiveth the prize? So, run that ye may obtain.*
> *And every man that striveth for the mastery is temperate in all things. Now they do it to obtain a corruptible crown; but we an incorruptible.*
> *I therefore so run, not as uncertainly; so fight I.*

But what is the end result if we choose *not* to run our race for God, but rather, we choose to acquiesce to every new trend, "every wind of doctrine" (Ephesians 4:14b)? In short, if left unfettered and unrestrained, the stronghold of comparison will *repeatedly* rear its ugly head and exert its invisible but nonetheless, seemingly insatiable tentacles into our lives. Such a choice ultimately results in a daunting, unmanageable impediment to our growth and likewise, circumvents all that our Father God has so lovingly and meticulously planned for each of our lives.

So, how do we effectively ward off entanglement in the comparison trap, when the often unspoken temptation, the invisible pressure to fit in, to be like others, relentlessly beckons us? How do we withstand those temptations and refrain from coveting what is not ours? Although God Himself may lovingly beckon, "Come out from among them and be ye separate…and touch not the unclean thing; and I will receive you" (2 Corinthians 6:17), at some point, at some time, our own inner need for acceptance may still entice us to give in, to succumb, to want to be like everyone else.

Granted, the biggest house, the finest clothes; the fastest, shiniest car; the praise of the crowds; etc. can be, oh so alluring. And for some, that is but a start…our want list could go on and on. That is, unless we stop it! Admittedly, it is far too easy to become enamored by what we see on television, the internet, or Facebook, etc. and to begin to think we are missing out or that we *deserve* these things, these supposed status symbols.

However, our Heavenly Father lovingly encourages us to "be content with such things as ye have, for he hath said, I will never leave you nor forsake you" (Hebrews 13:5). Regardless of what we acquire on this earth, once we have breathed our last breath, we can take none of it with us. As Job astutely pointed out, "Naked came I out of my mother's womb, and naked shall I return thither" (Job 1:21a). And, yet, despite the overarching truth and somber reality of these timeless words, the seductive appeal and false promises of comparison continue to entice.

For instance, television reality shows have captivated record audiences for years, which, in turn, has resulted in millions of dollars of additional revenue for the networks that sponsor them. One particularly popular reality show of yesteryear was *Extreme Makeover*, in which viewers, displeased with their physical appearance, wrote to the show to request consideration as possible contestants. If selected, they would undergo a radical makeover that usually required significant alteration to their physical appearance.

Undoubtedly, there were advantages to these makeovers. Once the plastic surgery and other medical procedures were performed, the contestant's hair professionally styled, an exhaustive overhaul of the outdated wardrobe accomplished, the results would be spectacular and breathtaking. The completely transformed contestant would often unabashedly shed tears of joy during the final unveiling before family, friends and the world.

Though never addressed on the weekly television show, after repeatedly viewing each final makeover contestant, week in and week out, one haunting, but never addressed issue continued to concern me. In short, *though outer transformation had undeniably occurred in each of the contestants, the inner person remained seemingly unchanged.* In a nutshell, though physically transformed, no emotional, mental or spiritual issues the individual may have been grappling with had been addressed. Instead, within at the very core and at the very fiber of their being, their identity, the essence of who they were appeared to remain the same—untouched. In fact, from a spiritual vantage point, the below scriptures further corroborate the criticality of this often overlooked, but essential perspective:

> *But the Lord said unto Samuel, Look not on his countenance, or on the height of his stature; because I have refused him: for the Lord seeth not as man seeth; for man looketh on the outward appearance, but the Lord looketh on the heart. (1 Samuel 16:7)*

> *Woe unto you, scribes and Pharisees, hypocrites! For ye are like unto whited sepulchres, which indeed appear beautiful outward, but are within full of dead men's bones, and of all uncleanness. (Matthew 23:27)*

> *Judge not according to the appearance, but judge righteous judgment. (John 7:24)*

> *For we commend not ourselves again unto you, but give you occasion to glory on our behalf, that ye may have somewhat to answer them which glory in appearance and not in heart. (2 Corinthians 5:12)*

> *Do ye look on things after the outward appearance? If any man trust to himself that he is Christ's let him of himself think this again, that, as he is Christ's, even so are we Christ's. (2 Corinthians 10:7)*

A seemingly common theme that runs throughout the aforementioned scriptures centers on the *fallacy* of placing undue emphasis only on the external, the tendency to only give credence and credibility to the *outer* man and to forego emphasis on or scrutiny of the *inner* man. Likewise, though each of us may undergo our own extreme makeover, such as new makeup, new hairstyle, new clothes, etc., and though an outwardly, beautiful exterior may emerge, it too remains temporal at best. In essence, all of us, no matter how beautiful we may appear outwardly—unless we die or undergo repeated cosmetic surgery—will eventually, with the passage of time, remain subject to the external aging process. As the Message Bible notes in Proverbs 31:30, "Charm can mislead and beauty soon fades."

Therefore to experience both inner and outer wholeness, it is paramount that we not overlook our *internal* need for an extreme makeover. Consequently, even if our external looks and beauty fade (and sooner or later they will, if we live long enough), we can yet remain confident and assured, like the Apostle Paul, that "though our outward man perish, yet the inward man is renewed day by day" (2 Corinthians 4:16).

Without doubt, inward renewal begins foremost with the rededication of our lives to our Lord and Savior, Jesus Christ (Romans 12:1, 2). In addition, to truly thrive and become all that God has called us to be, each of us may also benefit from transparent accountability via another family member, friend, trusted associate who, in the helter-skelter busyness of the often hectic, challenging, and seemingly endless demands of our lives, can provide a much-needed objective checks and balances or serve as a critical, trustworthy sounding board. Whether our problem is excessive spending, covetousness, overeating, etc., accountability can provide an essential and crucial underlying support system that congruently helps us navigate our successful escape from entanglement in the deceptive clutches of the comparison trap.

Not previously addressed, a significant root of our problem may not only stem from the unwise comparison of ourselves with others but also a corresponding diminution of our own attributes. For instance, ever consider the role of a staple? A staple—such a tiny object, and yet so essential when we are in search of one to hold our priceless documents or papers together. In that same vein, like a staple, our goal, mission, or purpose may be small and miniscule to the unassuming bystander, and yet it may play an immeasurable and indispensable role in the life of the one who most needs what only we can give. As we reflect once more on the woman with the issue of blood (discussed earlier in chapter 5 of this book), who, after spending all the monies she had on physicians who could provide her no answers, no physical relief and no healing from her longstanding, twelve-year old medical condition, nonetheless fought through immense crowds and the pressing throng surrounding Jesus Christ to get to Him. Scriptures note that, desperate, she reached out, if only to haltingly, briefly extend the tips of her fingers to touch the hem of His woolen garment (Matthew 9:20–22, Mark 5:25–34, Luke 8:43–48). On the outside, hers was a seemingly small, insignificant gesture, similar to the role that a simple staple plays. And yet that seemingly unimportant outward gesture—that is, touching the hem of our Savior's garment—denoted a gigantic leap of faith in which this woman's body was healed, her life never the same.

A common tendency is for us to categorize life, situations, and events into the big and the little, the large and the small, the significant and the insignificant and to often put much more emphasis on the tangible and what we can see rather than on the intangible and what is not visible to the eye. For instance, though our 401(k) (the visible) may appear to be diversified and to fare well by current market standards, our *spiritual* account (the invisible) may be bone dry. In fact, we may have never opened a *spiritual* account, as some of us may have never considered or even pondered *investments for eternity* (the invisible). However, Colossians 3:1 strongly encourages us to "set (our) affection on things above and not on things of the earth, where moth and rust break through and steal." Second Corinthians 4:18 further clarifies as it notes: "For the things which are seen, are temporal; but the things which are not seen, are eternal."

From a financial viewpoint, those who invested in Microsoft in the infancy of this company are now multimillionaires. Likewise, from a spiritual vantage point, those of us who are Christians and have given our lives to Christ have not only invested our lives into a kingdom not of this world, "an house not made with hands, eternal in the heavens" (2 Corinthians 5:1), but also in the glorious promise of eternal life with our Lord and Savior, Jesus Christ, as well. Unlike Microsoft investors, however, for some of us, on this side of glory, we may have experienced no tangible dividends, no corresponding rise in our spiritual bank accounts. Instead, we may continue to be plagued by ill health, meager finances, unstable familial relationships, and uncertain employment. And yet despite no visible guarantees, if we but keep our eyes on our Lord and Savior, Jesus Christ, our faith remains undaunted, our hope secure in our invisible, yet all-powerful, omniscient Father God. Our unwavering trust and belief in our Heavenly Father and in His promises continues to propel us forward. And though the long anticipated, promised outcome may not be apparent with the naked eye, we continue to invest our time, our energies, our resources, and ourselves as we march on in our spiritual walk, confident that we will see—if not in this life, then most assuredly in the eternal life that awaits us as believers—the results of a steadfast, unshakeable, immoveable faith in the living Christ, the Hope of Glory.

Without question, many of the material "treasures" of this earth do not last. Often, after much use and disuse, these treasures may even find their way to a yard sale, an auction, or even the junkyard. Many of us—some sooner, some later—have found that the "treasures" for which we clamored and that we *had to have* offered no deep, lasting satisfaction.

However, when we walk in devoted faith, trust, and obedience, in lockstep with our resurrected and steadfast Friend, our Lord and Savior, Jesus Christ, we are promised an eternal legacy. When we deliberately choose *not* to embroil ourselves in comparison and choose *not* to compare ourselves to others, doing so cannot only have profound implications for us but, as briefly mentioned earlier in this work, also powerfully impact our children and our children's children as we intentionally encourage them to embrace their own uniqueness and to rejoice in who God made each of them to be. In other words, we don't have to travel alone; but our God extends a warm, loving welcome to our family, to our friends and to all others as well, if they choose to follow Jesus Christ. The invitation is to "all that are afar off, even as many as the Lord our God shall call" (Acts 2:39). Perhaps not emphasized enough, our God is a multigenerational God. Not only is He the God of Abraham, Isaac, and Jacob (Matthew 22:32);

but the import that God places on family is displayed throughout the multiple genealogies recorded in the Bible.

Note, for example, that the first chapter of Matthew traces our Lord and Savior, Jesus Christ, down through forty-two generations. In Deuteronomy 6:7, and again in Deuteronomy 11:19, God makes specific reference to our progeny, as he commands, "And thou shalt teach them diligently unto thy children and shall talk of them while thou sittest in thine house, and thou walkest by the way and when thou liest down and when thou risest up" (Deuteronomy 6:7). Revelation 22:17 aptly sums up our Lord's open and loving invitation to *all* of humanity: "And the Spirit and the bride say, Come. And let him that heareth say, Come. And let him that is athirst come. And whosoever will, let him take the water of life freely."

God's admonition to us as parents has always been to hand down His statutes, laws, and teachings to our children and to our children's children, transmitted from generation to generation to ensure a godly legacy of unique individuals with unique, God-given gifts, talents, and abilities. God believes in and advocates such legacy, initially promising Abraham, "Look now toward heaven, and tell the stars, if thou be able to number them: and he said unto him, So shall thy seed be" (Genesis 15:5), and later, promising Isaac that He would "multiply thy seed for my servant Abraham's sake" (Genesis 26:24). And to each of us, our Father God also promised "the man that feareth the Lord, that delighteth greatly in his commandments, *his seed* shall be mighty upon earth; the *generation of the upright* shall be blessed" (Psalm 112:1–2, italics, mine). Our striving to make a God-inspired, God-honoring difference in the lives of others and to *not* compare ourselves to others but follow our own God-given pathway can not only significantly impact us, but our progeny and multiple others as well, throughout the entirety of our lives and even after we are gone.

In the not-so-distant past, if a man worked for a company for thirty to forty years, he might receive a gold watch and a small pension at retirement. But even those seemingly small tokens of recognition could not possibly encompass the true value or magnitude of dedication, sacrifice, and diligence that that employee may have given to his organization over the several decades he actually labored on his job. Glimpsed through society's often faulty, inequitable lens of *comparison with others*, that now older gentleman may or may not have achieved any significant level of success by man's standards. And yet, God knows His divine plan for this man's life. And God not only knows how hard this man worked on his earthly job, but also how much he sacrificed or gave in service to our Lord. The Bible assures each of us that "your labor is not in vain in the Lord" (1 Corinthians 15:58). For that reason, we must not be weary in well-doing (Galatians 6:9). Though others may or may not appreciate our hard work or labor of love, there is One who declares that our reward is with Him and that He will reward us in that final Day (Isaiah 40:10, Revelation 22:12).

And, so, under the guiding hand of our Eternal Father, it is up to each of us to make our own distinct, indelible mark in this world. Rather than please others or compare our achievements with theirs, it is up to us to complete the distinct mission that Jesus Christ has given to you and that He has given to me.

For that is what God asks of us—to be the unique and distinct, one-of-a-kind individuals He has called each of us to be *in Him*. As 1 Peter 2:9 proclaims, "But ye are a chosen generation, a royal priesthood, an holy nation, a peculiar people; that ye should shew forth the praises of him who hath called you out of darkness into his marvelous light." Granted, we are alike in that we are all made in God's image. And though each of us is also vastly different, each of us is esteemed, treasured, called apart, and significant in the eyes of our Maker. So the real question becomes *Can you and I rejoice today in our uniqueness, in who Father God made you to be and in who He made me to be?* In all the world, there will never be another you, and there will never be another me.

I can stop looking. You can stop looking. The search is over! It all begins and ends with Jesus Christ, for it is He for whom our hearts have searched and pined. He is the only one who can fill the void, the emptiness, the hole in our hearts. He is your righteousness. He is my love. He is your truth. We may look the world over, but you and I need look no further. We need not look outside of ourselves or to anyone or to anything else. The striving is over. Christ is the author and finisher of our faith (Hebrews 12:2). Christ is our righteousness (1 Corinthians 1:30, 2 Corinthians 5:21). You and I don't have to be "good enough" anymore. Because of His shed blood on Calvary, He has made you and He has made me more than enough. You don't have to strive; I don't have to measure up. You and I are His pride and joy, the apple of His eye, hidden under the shadow of His wings (Psalm 17:8). Our Heavenly Father God, who cannot lie (Numbers 23:19), lovingly reminds us in His Word that, as His children, Christ can accomplish in us and through us that which He has purposed for each of us since the beginning of Creation, if we are yielded to Him. And, if we but remain faithful to Him, we can rejoice, even now in what He will bring to pass in our lives.

Yes, even now, we can unabashedly celebrate what God has given others, while we also congruently celebrate what God has given to you and to me. Without doubt, there remains immense indescribable satisfaction in doing what God has called you and me to do and to be. Therefore, rather than appease or please other people, we can strive to please only one… Father God. To awaken every day reminding ourselves of what God says about us and who God made each of us to be is its own best prescription for self-esteem.

As you and I navigate the corridors of life, may we consider holding our possessions loosely, for all we have ultimately belongs to God. To briefly revisit the story of Abraham, God gave Abraham what he really wanted—a son. But God then asked Abraham to give his son back to Him. Without even questioning Father God, Abraham obediently and unflinchingly placed his most precious gift from God (his only son), on the altar. Abraham had to give up his own dreams of legacy to obey God. But God responded to Abraham's indisputable act of faith, noting that "thou fearest God, seeing thou hast not withheld thy son, thine only son from me" (Genesis 22:12). And as a result of Abraham's steadfast, unwavering faith in God and his willingness to give up what he most loved (his son), God rewarded Abraham with the promise that "in thy seed shall all the nations of the earth be blessed; because thou hast obeyed my voice" (Genesis 22:18).

In this life, when it is so easy to become embroiled in the comparison trap, to strive to emulate and to please others, to want to be accepted and to be a part of the crowd, we must intentionally remind ourselves that we actually perform for an audience of one. This, in turn, further raises yet another question: *Am I pleasing the One who matters most?*

For, truly, it is God who causes us to triumph (2 Corinthians 2:14). It is He who causes us to prosper (Deuteronomy 8:18). Our loud displays, our pomp and circumstance make no difference to the One who matters most. It is what God thinks and says about us that really matters. God forbid that we follow in the footsteps of the Pharisees, of whom John wrote, "For they loved the praises of men more than the praise of God" (John 12:43).

The battle to victory may not be easy and may be fraught with setbacks! And yet, freedom from the comparison trap *mandates* that each of us purposely embrace our own, God-assigned, God-directed marching orders. As He distributes to each of us varying talents and abilities, your marching orders may not resemble mine, nor will mine resemble yours.

For instance, the disciple Luke recounts in Acts 16: 25-26, the challenging marching orders of Paul and Silas who, while *bound* and *imprisoned*, began to praise God. As they did so, there was a great earthquake. Not only were their bands loosed, but the bands of all those imprisoned with them were suddenly loosed as well. Why would they sing and praise God while *chained* and during the *darkest* part of night? Clearly unimpeded by shackles of comparison or by what others might think or say, perhaps it was because they knew in whom they unabashedly believed (2 Timothy 1:12) and they no doubt took comfort and joy in knowing that they were in the center of God's will and that He was able to keep them from falling (Jude 24).

Amid our own hard-fought battles, it is time to celebrate and embrace who God made you to be and who He made me to be: a masterpiece, a one of a kind, without equal, without match—a priceless original. It is time to give to God what only you and I can give. It is time to defiantly refuse the inclination to compare ourselves to another or to pine for or covet what someone else may easily, unabashedly proffer. Instead, it is time to celebrate, to be who only you can be, to be who only I can be. Give only what you can give for you are fearfully and wonderfully made (Psalm 139:14), and there is no one else in all the world quite like you or quite like me.

In the beloved church I attended growing up, there was an old congregational spiritual we used to sing. The words of the song declared, "Ninety-nine, Lord, ninety-nine, Lord / ninety-nine and a half won't do / ninety-nine, Lord, ninety-nine, Lord / ninety-nine and a half won't do." Within scholarly circles, "ninety-nine and a half" is almost a perfect grade, an A-plus, by most standards. However, when it comes to pleasing God and living for Him, this song resonated its own underlying yet powerful message that complete, total surrender was the *only* way to please God. And as noted in scripture, God wants 100 percent, *all* of us. In Revelation 3:15–16, our Lord and Savior, Jesus Christ, declares that, for those who are lukewarm, He will spue them out of His mouth. But, conversely, what happens when we give Him our *all?* In 2 Chronicles 15:12, Scripture clearly records, "And they entered into a covenant to seek the Lord God of their fathers with *all* their heart, and with *all* their soul." Just a few verses later, in 2 Chronicles 15:15, "All Judah rejoiced at the oath; for they had sworn with *all* their heart, and sought him with their *whole* desire, and *he was found of them and the Lord gave them rest round about*" (italics mine).

And yet, despite such comforting reassurance in the previous scripture, during certain times in our lives, the validation, acceptance, and approval we seek from others may not come. The psalmist David may have experienced a similar situation, but after he turned his gaze to Almighty God, he confidently penned the words, "Truly, my soul waiteth upon God: *from Him* cometh my salvation. He *only* is my rock and my salvation; he is my defense; I shall not be greatly moved "(Psalm 62:1–2, italics, mine).

Like David, we must each ultimately look to our Lord and Savior, Jesus Christ, for validation and affirmation. It is incumbent upon each of us to strive to be who God called each of us to be and *not* yearn or covet to be someone or something else. Each of us matters, each of us is priceless and invaluable in the eyes of our Heavenly Father.

On a final note, we remind ourselves that "God is no respecter of persons" (Acts 10:34). He does *not* categorize or judge us by race, skin color, ethnicity, class, social standing, personality, talent, ability, etc. Instead, our Heavenly Father highly esteems each of us and views each of us as His priceless original. He who made the differences in each of us, delights in those differences and in what makes each of us *exceptional.* He did not create us to compare ourselves to another, to outdo another or to covet what another may possess.

Rather, we were created to glorify our Lord and Savior, Jesus Christ, to become what only you and I can uniquely become and to give what only you and I can uniquely give. So, yes, it is time for victorious celebration! For there is no one else like you or like me. Distinct, unparalleled, incomparable masterpieces—that is you and that is me! Our Heavenly Father loves each of us (John 3:16)!

Prayer

Lord, help me to realize who You made me to be. Let me cast off the inaccurate definitions that others may have of me. And instead, help me to boldly embrace my own unapologetic definition and description of myself penned by God Himself. Lord, help me to have my own internal "standard," my own "benchmark" as defined by Father God…of who You made me to be and what You created me to do. And, in that process, help me to be the best me that I can be and not permit myself to be defined by the erroneous standard or definition of another. Help me to celebrate who You made me to be, even if it means that I go upstream in a downstream world, as Caleb (Joshua 14:11–12) and Joshua (Joshua 24:15) did.

And lastly, dear Lord, as I break free and stay free from continued entanglement in the comparison trap, help me to remember that my history does not determine my destiny. Help me to celebrate who I am in You! Thank you, Lord, that I forget those things which are behind, reach forth unto those things that are before me and steadfastly press toward the mark for the prize of the high calling of God in Christ Jesus (Philippians 3:13–14). And it is in the magnificent, unrivaled name of my Lord and Savior, Jesus Christ, that I pray and commit my life, my hopes, my dreams, and all that I am to You always. Amen.

The Comparison Trap: How to Break Free, How to Stay Free

For we dare not make ourselves of the number, or compare ourselves with some that commend themselves: but they measuring themselves by themselves, and comparing themselves among themselves are not wise.
—2 Corinthians 10:12

THE PREMISE OF *THE COMPARISON Trap: How to Break Free, How to Stay Free* is to challenge each reader to identify the comparison trap for what it is—an entanglement, a false diversion from the powerful plan and life of destiny that Christ ultimately wants to ignite in each of our lives (Jeremiah 29:11). And while undoubtedly extricating ourselves from the binding stronghold of comparison is a cogent first step, the foremost question remains: Can each of us feasibly step away from the discarded grave clothes of *comparison*, hopefully now lying on the ground about us, and passionately, with unreserved abandon and unbridled passion, *stay free* of comparison and begin to embark upon a lifelong, focused pursuit of God's singular, distinct design and purpose for each of our lives?

As you may recall from earlier chapters in this book, several poignant steps to wrest ourselves from the comparison trap were mentioned and are again recapped below:

- *To extricate ourselves from the comparison trap mandates that we purposely weed through what we previously considered so important and so urgent, that is, our "must haves," and begin to earnestly identify what is truly needful in our lives, but this time, intently examined within the penetrating, illuminating light of God's Word.*
- *To flee the comparison trap requires the tenacity to deliberately recognize and embrace our uniqueness and what makes each of us who we are.*
- *To successfully exit the comparison trap necessitates acceptance of the indisputable truth that only Father God can meet our deepest needs.*
- *To successfully wrest ourselves from the comparison trap demands that we intentionally, purposely refuse to imitate or adopt the attributes, traits, qualities, etc. that God has bestowed on others as the "gold standard" for our own success.*

Inevitably, in the wake of our own insecurity and doubt, questions such as *Who am I? Am I good enough? Why am I here? Why don't I measure up?* etc. may arise. Yet an often overlooked yet critical question is never considered. In short, to ask ourselves this poignant, introspective question is an effective strategy and the first step necessary to circumvent a *return* to the comparison trap. The crucial, introspective question? *What was I thinking about in the first place that prompted a comparison of myself with another?*

In addition to the above first step, to effectively avoid a *return* to the comparison trap also encompasses the below steps 2 through 4, presented earlier in this book:

- *The second step to avoid a return to the comparison trap lies in our verbal communication (to include self-talk) as we deliber-*

ately replace destructive words and lingering self-doubts with the infallible, unerring truth of God's Word.

- *The third step to avoid a return to the comparison trap lies in forgiving others. Why? Because when we do so, you and I give ourselves a "gift" as we purposefully take back the power we previously gave those who offended us when we initially refused to release them from the strongholds they may have held in our lives.*
- *The fourth step to avoid a return to the comparison trap is to wisely assess when to speak and when to remain silent.*

But, even if you and I adhere to the four previously mentioned steps, is such a plan of action *enough* for us to *stay free* from the allure of the comparison trap? In short, the answer to this question is an unequivocal yes, *but only* when our Father God can venture into those parts of you and of me that we *permit* Him to enter. The scripture proclaims, "*That I might know Him* and the power of his resurrection, and the *fellowship* of his sufferings, being made conformable unto his death" (Philippians 3:10, italics, mine). Contrarily, *not* knowing Him, *not* walking in intimacy with Him, precludes me from experiencing "the depths of the riches both of the wisdom and knowledge of God" (Romans 11:33) and walking in the freedom Christ offers each of us.

I once heard Kathy Hayes, wife of Pastor Mike Hayes, pastor emeritus of Covenant Church in Carrollton, Texas, break down the definition of the word *intimacy* into a very easy-to-enunciate and easily understood quadrisyllabic phrase: "in to me see." And that is what intimacy denotes: allowing someone else to see us as we really are. My husband and I have been married for over forty years now, and I have been blessed with the best husband in the world. He is so loving and trustworthy. However, no matter how long we have been married, if I keep parts of myself from my husband, or he keeps parts of himself from me, I can never know him or he, me, in the depths of intimacy that God originally designed for us as husband and wife. So, it is in our relationship with God.

If our Father God could be described in one word, it would be "love." His Love is far-reaching, indescribable, and incomprehensible. We may think we love our spouse, children, our parents, our siblings, our friends, and other dear ones, but our love in no way encompasses God's rich, unfathomable, longsuffering love for each of us. In fact, His love is so limitless that many cannot accept it as real. They cannot believe that someone would love them, with all the lies, with all the heinous actions, unspeakable atrocities they may have said and done, and yet Jesus Christ loved them and willingly dared to die on Calvary's cross for them. Moreover, Jesus Christ continues to extend His nail-pierced hands and to beckon, "Come unto me, all ye that labour and are heavy laden, and I will give you rest" (Matthew 11:28). In fact, the Bible admonishes, "How shall we escape, if we neglect so *great* salvation" (Hebrews 2:3, italics mine).

When a homeowner wants to sell his house, he will usually put a "For Sale" sign in the front yard or advertise his property in a real estate listing. This alerts perspective buyers that his property is available. However, when an owner has not listed his property, and an inquiring buyer is intrigued by the house so much that he wants to buy it, since it is not for sale, the owner would probably ward off the unwelcome buyer's pursuits or unsolicited offers.

So it is with God's love, only God's love is available and the *purchase price* is simply accepting Him into our hearts as our Lord and Savior and, in turn, giving our *all* to Him. But like the unwelcome buyer, you and I can't *buy* God's love. It's not about our works, our performance, or how many people you and I bring to the Lord. Rather, it's all about the personal relationship that each of us has with our risen Lord and Savior. We never have to buy or earn His love. No work we do, no amount of service we give, can ever replace the ultimate price He paid for us when He gave His life on Calvary's cross.

Though certainly not as plenteous as they once were, the often hand-painted, endearing "Just Married" signs, complete with streamers of empty beverage cans on the back fender of the newlywed's car, often evokes pleasant images, memories, or even a faint smile for many of us.

Though it may be hard to sometimes envision or grasp, when we choose to accept Christ into our lives, we become *married* to Jesus Christ. Unlike some today who may not embrace the "till death do us part" concept of marriage, when we accept Christ as our Lord and Savior, He is wedded to us. In fact, He hates divorce from His children (Malachi 2:16) so much that Scripture says that He is married to the backslider (Jeremiah 3:14). As previously mentioned, several times throughout this book, God's ever binding, marital promise to each of us is "I will never leave you nor forsake you" (Hebrews 13:5).

With such promises, you and I need only realize that God is our *faithful husband and lover* and that He has placed His ring on our finger and does not have a wandering eye. Lamentations 3:23b reminds us, "Great is (His) faithfulness." Thus, there is nothing and no one in this world that can ever separate us from the love that God has for each of us (Romans 8: 38–39).

What is so wonderful about the Word of God, the Bible, is that it represents an unconditional compendium of His love for you, for me, and for all of mankind. As our Savior and dearest friend, even when we don't get it right, He promises to never desert us (Isaiah 43:2-4). Though He does not condone or approve our bad behaviors, misdeeds, or our poor decisions, His love for us remains steadfast and unconditional. Such knowledge and assurance encourages us to find our rest in Him.

Solitude, mentioned earlier in this book, can often be fertile ground for *intimacy* with God. As there were numerous times in Scripture when our Lord deliberately sought solitude to commune with His Father (Matt. 14:23; Mark. 1:35; Luke. 9:18), so must we. There is something that is so quietly refreshing about time spent alone with God. There is also something that is calmly reassuring about resting in God and taking life *one day at a time*. And though you and I still wisely plan, we can now deliberately resist the urge for self-absorption where our plans and our goals suddenly take center stage, with no thought of Father God's will and His goals for us. Instead of "Let my will be done," we can begin to intentionally follow Father God's admonition to let His "will be done in earth as it is in heaven" (Matthew 6:10).

Now, newly armed with the strategies to *break free* and *stay free* from the comparison trap, what happens if you and I fail and once again become embroiled in the tangled web of comparison? In response to this question, allow me to conclude this work with a final word—the mention of *God's grace*, His unmerited favor. As with all children, when our now adult sons were growing up, they sometimes got into mischief and did things they should not have done. Though my husband and I may have been understandably upset at their antics or wrongdoing, we never disowned them, no matter the infraction. Why? Because no matter their misdeeds, they were still our sons, our offspring, our legacy, flesh of our flesh and bone of our bone. They would always be Copelands and would always belong to our family. We could not and would never give up on them because we love and adore them! God's Word says that if we (mere men and women), being evil, know how to give good gifts to our children, "how much more shall your Father which is in heaven give good things to them that ask him?" (Matthew 7:11)

Let's face it. None of us will ever be *good enough* to go to heaven. That is what is so wonderful about God's grace. His grace frees us from the comparison trap or the need to be man pleasers. Instead, we now seek to please only One, our Abba Father; and when we don't measure up—that is, we make the wrong decision and we blow it—we have an advocate with the Father, our Lord and Savior, Jesus Christ, who forgives us and is praying for us. Who couldn't love a God like that?

And, though, we *work out* our own salvation with fear and trembling (Philippians 2:12, italics mine), God's *gift* of salvation is free. None of us can *work* our way to heaven; none of us can work to *earn* God's favor. Rather, God's invitation is "whomsoever will, let him come" (Mark 8:34–38; Rev. 22:17). Each of us has an "inheritance" already established and set aside for us by our Heavenly Father (Col. 1:12–14).

Rather than embrace comparison and assume the characteristics, dress, personality, etc., of another, the overarching message of *The Comparison Trap: How to Break Free, How to Stay Free* is to challenge each of us to consider a far more enduring life goal. That life goal? To maintain our distinct individuality; to fulfill our own singularly, unique, God-given purpose; and most of all, to reflect our Lord and Savior, Jesus Christ, in our thoughts, in our words, in our actions…in sum, in our lives. When we refuse to remain entangled in the comparison trap, *we break free*. When we no longer permit the thoughts, words, and actions of others to define us, we *stay free*. And when we both *break free* and *stay free* of the comparison trap we, in essence, give our Father God permission to divinely navigate the course and the direction of our lives. And when we do so, like the Apostle Paul, we, too, can unequivocally declare, "Follow me as I follow Christ" (1 Corinthians 11:1).

"As God has distributed to each one, as the Lord has called each one, so let him walk" (1 Corinthians 7:17).

Prayer

Dear Heavenly Father, In the mighty, all-powerful, healing name of Jesus Christ, completely tear down the stranglehold of comparison in my life, never to be resurrected again, so that You and You alone are my God and so that I have no other gods before You. Having discarded and laid aside the chains of comparison, let me choose to move beyond the crowd, beyond what others may or may not say, beyond the need for approval, beyond the naysayers and beyond the man-pleasing and instead, let me choose to accomplish great things for You, my Lord and my Savior, Jesus Christ.

Help me to surrender my life, my dreams, my future, and who I am to Your divine plan and Your divine will for my life. Let me die to myself and live to You, for as Your Word states, "Except a corn of wheat fall into the ground and die, it abideth alone but, if it die, it bringeth forth much fruit" (John 12:24).

Help me to march to the beat of a different drummer, Lord, and fulfill Your purpose for my life, for I am no longer my own but have been brought with a price, that I might glorify You in my body and in my spirit, which are God's (1 Corinthians 6:20).

Lord, help me to live in such a way that I do not look to man for my reward but to You. Come in and dine with me, Lord Jesus, so that I may know You intimately (Philippians 3:10). Fill all of the empty places in my heart and in my life with You.

Finally, may You alone always receive the glory, honor, and praise in my life, my Savior, my Lord, my dearest, my most cherished Friend! It is in the matchless name of my Lord and Savior, Jesus Christ, I pray. Amen.

If the Son therefore shall make you free, ye shall be free indeed. (John 8:36)

ABOUT THE AUTHOR

YVONNE COPELAND RECEIVED HER BACHELOR'S degree in sociology from Davidson College, her master's degree in administration from Central Michigan University, and her master's degree in social work from the University of Texas-Arlington. A licensed clinical social worker (LCSW), the author's past sixteen years in the field of social work have included intense, hands-on experience in inpatient and outpatient mental health settings at the state and federal levels of government, respectively.

Ms. Copeland's drive and passion to treat those with behavioral health issues stem from her work with patients from all walks of life, from those with severe mental illness (SMI) to the mildly impaired, to veterans, to those in the general population. As a result of her extensive work experience, Ms. Copeland has observed that while the often-overlooked concept of unwise comparison can sometimes assume a minor role in those who struggle with behavioral health issues, at other times, it may represent a root cause.

The Comparison Trap: How to Break Free, How to Stay Free combines both the author's education and extensive mental health work experience with her steadfast belief in the power and inerrancy of God's Word as the foundation and guiding force in all of life.

Ms. Copeland currently works in private practice where she provides therapy to patients experiencing mental health challenges. Though *The Comparison Trap: How to Break Free, How to Stay Free* marks her first book, the author has previously penned several published works of nonfiction.

9 781638 740186